The Blessed Death of Those Who Die in the Lord

Discoursed in seven searching, but very sweet sermons
on Revelation 14:13, wherein several weighty cases
relating to death in general, and to dying in the
Lord in particular, are succinctly, solidly,
and satisfyingly handled

by

James Durham

Preacher of the Gospel in Glasgow

"All the days of my appointed time will I wait, till my
change come." Job 14:14

"So teach us to number our days, that we may
apply our hearts to wisdom." Psalm 90:12

Edited by Dr. Don Kistler

Soli Deo Gloria Publications
. . . *for instruction in righteousness* . . .

Soli Deo Gloria Publications
A division of Soli Deo Gloria Ministries, Inc.
P. O. Box 451, Morgan, PA 15064
(412) 221-1902/FAX 221-1902
www.SDGbooks.com

*

*

ISBN 1-57358-152-6

Library of Congress Cataloging-in-Publication Data

Durham, James, 1622-1658.
  [Blessednesse of the death of these that die in the Lord]
  The blessed death of those who die in the Lord / by James Durham;
edited by Don Kistler.
     p. cm.
  ISBN 1-57358-152-6
  1. Bible. N.T. Revelation XIV, 13–Sermons. 2. Presbyterian
  Church–Sermons. 3. Sermons, English–Scotland. I. Kistler, Don.
  II. Title.
BS2825.54 .D87 2003
252'.052–dc21
                                          2003009914

Contents

To the Christian Reader

Christian Reader,

Many and various are the vicissitudes and changes to which sin has sadly subjected us poor, transient, itinerate, miserable mortals, grieving, groaning, dwining, and decaying nothings; the rear-reward of all which changes is at length brought up by death, that last, great, and vastly momentous change, which puts a final period to all the changes that shall ever befall us in this world; and whereby every one of us without exception of sex, age, descent, degree, calling, or capacity will be put into an eternally unchangeable state of happiness or of misery. If so, then surely it is very sad, and never enough to be lamented, if it were with tears of blood, that men and women who have rational and immortal souls endued with a discurring faculty, and capable of eternal happiness in the enjoyment of God, and of eternal misery in separation and destruction from His presence, should for the most part so much abstract from the serious thoughts of that most important change, followed with so long a train of everlastingly concerning consequences, and in their retired meditations, take so few turns in this long gallery of eternity, as if all that the divinely inspired Scriptures say of it, and that many every day experience the truth of, were a mere romance, or cunningly devised fable.

And yet, notwithstanding, death is most incontrovertibly certain, all men being by divine appointment concluded under a necessity of dying; which appointment takes in not only the infallible certainty of the thing, but the determination of the precise time, when; of the place, where; and of the manner, how; whither by a violent or natural death, whither by a more sudden

iv

and surprising, or by a more lent and lingering death.
For our times are in the hand of the Lord; the years,
months, weeks, days, and moments of them, with all
their incident changes and revolutions, are at His disposal. There is an appointed time to man on earth. God
has determined the times before appointed; the times
and seasons are kept in the Father's own power. Our
days are determined, and the number of our months is
with Him. He has set bounds to us which we cannot
transgress. There is no possibility of circumducing the
day prefixed to the continuance of our life by His appointment.

This is not at all gainsaid by what the Psalmist says
of bloody and deceitful men. He says that they shall not
live out half their days, that is, they shall often not live
half or nearly so long as they might according to the
ordinary course of nature, or not half or near so long as
they desired, designed, and expected. Or, they shall be
cut off in the throng of their business, and in the midst
of their projects and designs; nor by that sentence of
death of a disease mortal in its own nature denounced
against King Hezekiah, and the addition of fifteen
years to his life, which imports only the change and reverse of a tacitly conditional commutation and sentence (as in that against the Ninevites, and that against
Abimelech in the matter of Sarai); but this is no
change at all of God's purpose and decree, who is not
as man that He should repent, whose counsel stands,
and with whom there is no variableness nor shadow of
turning; who had decreed in His eternal purpose that
drawing forth Hezekiah's life that length, and who had
by His decree infallibly ensured the performance of the
condition—to wit, Hezekiah praying, humbling himself, and rousing up of himself yet more to the serious
exercise of godliness, and his using prescribed means
for the recovery of his health.

Nor is it gainsaid by any other Scripture rightly understood. So it seems to be (to say no worse) atheological, and not at all consistent with divine Scripture dictates, positively and peremptorily, to deny that the outmost term and period of this mortal life is unalterably fixed in the eternal purpose of God. It is very unreasonable to subtract and exempt so concerning and important a thing as the last term of a man's life, or the precise time of his death, which in the Scripture is by way of eminency above and beyond all other changes called his "change," even that whereby he steps over the border of time into eternity, from the sovereign influence of His decree and of His Providence who most vigilantly and accurately inspects the infrustratable execution thereof; since they teach the least momentous and most minute things, even the numbering of our hairs, and the falling of a sparrow to the ground.

Besides, whatever is or can be said against this seems with equal strength to militate against the immutability of the divine purposes and decrees about the everlasting state of men, and to infer as great an uncertainty of the latter as of the former. Indeed, it is worthy of observation that those who most violently maintain (I say "most violently" because I know there are some other orthodox men who demur this) that the term of human life is unfixed, mutable, and ambulatory, even in the eternal decree and foreknowledge of God, as well as it is contingent and uncertain in respect of natural and second causes. They also patronize and peremptorily plead for the mutability and conditionality (for both come to the same amount) of God's decrees about men's spiritual and everlasting state, making Him either daily to acquire new knowledge, though known to Him are all His works from the beginning, or at least to be doubtful and unresolved in His purposes till new emergents arising from an uncontrolled and self-governing free will causes Him to take new measures and resolutions. This is a doctrine justly exploded by all truly orthodox divines as being unworthy of, and injurious to, the infinitely wise and absolutely supreme Governor of the world. This opinion has a tendency (however it may be plastered over with specious and splendid pretenses of something else) to narrow and limit the sovereign dominion and will of the infinite majesty of God the Creator so that the will of the finite and futile creature may have the greater scope and latitude of liberty; which yet is no liberty indeed, nor worthy of the name of liberty, because it is not that wherewith the Son of God makes free. This takes the crown of the glory of the conversion and salvation of sinners off the head of free grace, and sets it most sacrilegiously on the head of their own lord, paramount free will. Also, it is in downright contradiction to the Scriptures of truth to make poor man proudly boast that it is not God, but he himself, who has made him to differ from others; and that he is more obliged in the matter of his conversion and salvation to his own toward, tractable, gentle, courteous, compliant, and obsequious free will than to God's decree of election, and the efficacious, omnipotently sweet, and sweetly omnipotent, infallibly and necessarily will-inclining and determining, though not forcibly violenting or compulsorily co-acting, influencing of sovereignly free grace.

If wantonly curious, superciliously insolent, tumultuously mutinous, corrupt human reason (ambitiously affecting to take up and comprehend the great abyss, and shoreless, bottomless, and incomprehensible ocean of the decrees and Providence of God within its own little and shallow cockleshell capacity) would suffer itself to be sobered and be calmed into a humble and just consideration of things, all those high and haughty reasonings and debatings against the unalterable fixedness of the last term of man's natural life, and against the immutability of His decrees in reference to their spiritual and everlasting state, would quickly be let fall; for then it would easily see the great congruity, and pleasing suitableness that is in subjecting all, and particularly the rational creatures being but derivate and borrowed bits of being from that first fountain, and original Being, that Being of beings, in all the events that befall them, and in all their motions, actings, and operations, according to their respective natures, entitatively, morally, or graciously good; and all the adhering anomies, ataxias, and vitiosities of them to the majesty of the most high God, as to His efficient producing of the one, and as to His permitting, bounding, ordering, and directing of the other, to His own holy and blessed ends, without being justly chargeable with the least culpable accession to them; who is, by the most absolute perfection of His purest nature, infinitely removed from all possibility of being reached by any tincture or touch of pollution.

It would also see clearly the most profoundly and admirably wise connection that in these decrees of God, and in the execution of them by His providence, is ordered between the ends, and all the several means leading thereto; it being evident beyond all hazard of rational contradiction that the boundary of the life of Ahab, and of that unbelieving Samaritan lord who was trodden to death in the gate of Samaria, and of our blessed Lord Jesus Himself, was determinately prefixed, since it was expressly foretold, as the Scripture clears. And it is simply impossible that divine predictions can prove false. Yet the man who shot at Ahab acted freely in so doing. Those who trampled that lord to death were not forced by any to gather themselves together into such a crowd, or to be so regardless of a person of honor. The murderers of Christ were not a whit less guilty for doing nothing but what God's hand and counsel determined before to be done, nor yet did our Lord anything that was irrational or foolish in using lawful and fit means for His own preservation, in so frequently retiring and hiding Himself from the Jews' violence as He did—even though, as the Scripture often makes mention, His hour was not yet come. By these instances it is very clear that the determinateness of the decrees of God in no way does violence to or infringes upon the native freedom of the wills of men; nor yet is it any excuse for their sin, or encouragement to their neglect of means, since it is by using rightly or neglecting these that God causes His unalterable decrees to take their designed effect.

As then it is most indubitably certain that we must die, so the time for the continuance of our life and days here is very short, even but as a handbreadth, and our age as nothing before Him. Our days are spent as a tale that is told; they are as a shadow on the earth, and there is none abiding. They are swifter than a post; they flee away and see no good; they are passed away as the swift ships, as the eagle that hastens to the prey. They are swifter than a weaver's shuttle; our life is even as a vapor that appears for a little time and then vanishes away as a little warm breath, that is turned in and out at our nostrils, which is very easily and quickly stopped. The precise time also of the expiring of this breath of life is (however to God, to whom are known all His works from the beginning) most infallibly certain, though to us most uncertain.

Death comes on us ordinarily in such an hour as we do not think of. It comes on us as "a thief in the night." We are now strong and in good health, and all of a sudden we grow weak and sickly. Now we live, and by and by we die, and see men no more in the land of the living. All which—to wit, the certainty of our death, the

exceeding brevity of our frail and brittle life, with the
great uncertainty of the precise time of our being—
with one voice unanimously call aloud to us seriously to
mind, and with all our might, to make for another life;
to make sure peace and friendship with God through
the blood of Christ's cross; to secure an interest in Him
(the choice of all interests, the only everlastingly
durable interest, in comparison of which all other interests are but petty and inconsiderable, to which they
all ought to cede and give place, and, as it were, to
strike their flag and lower their topsail) by sincerely
closing with Jesus Christ on His own terms, and cordially consenting to, and taking hold of, the Covenant
of Grace; and to live so as it becomes them, who are very
certain that we shall die, and very uncertain how long
we shall live.

We should endeavor through grace to have our
loins girded, to have our affections, as it were, trussed
up so that they may not hang down and trail on the
earth, and to have our lights burning; not only to make
sure on solid and good grounds that we have a stock of
habitual grace, but to endeavor to have it lively and vigorous in its exercise, even burning into a flame; that we
may be as men who wait for the coming of their Lord,
so that in whatsoever watch He shall come, we may be
ready to open to Him immediately, even at the very first
knock, were it on a night's, a day's, or an hour's, yea,
were it but on a moment's warning, having our house
in such order, and the spiritual affairs of our souls so
well disposed of, and in so good a posture and case,
that we may not be taken tardy or napping, nor be suddenly and sadly surprised to our unspeakable prejudice;
even to be in that most desirable and delightful condition that to us to live may be Christ, that the very prin-
cipal scope and end which we propose to ourselves in
desiring life and health may be the honor and glory of

Jesus Christ. We are to be looking at life, with all the external conveniences and comforts of it, as but little valuable, and unworthy to be desired were it not mainly in order to this end.

Then we may confidently and comfortably conclude that death—whenever, wherever, and however it should overtake us—would be gain to us, by putting a final and eternal period to all the remainders of indwelling sin, to all temptations to sin, to all desertion, and to all complaints and fears of desertion and hidings of God's face; to all doubtings about our gracious estate and about our interest in God; to all fears of backsliding, and of offending or of giving offence; to all trouble, sorrow, sadness, and sighing on whatsoever account; to all indisposition to serve, worship, and glorify God; to all interruptions of fellowship with Him, and to all fellowship that is but mediate and in part; to all sinful ignorance and imperfect knowledge, or that which is but in part. In heaven, great theologians read all their divinity without books, and without the least difficulty in that beatifical immediate vision of God's face. Death ushers us in to that blessed state wherein we shall be satisfied with His likeness, and that both objectively and subjectively, being then admitted to see Him in Himself as He is, face to face, even to full, immediate, and never-to-be-interrupted fellowship with Him. Then we will be privileged to see Him in ourselves, perfectly conformed to His image in holiness according to creature capacity; and put in case to serve Him there, where His servants serve Him as well as ever we desired to serve Him in the best frames we were ever in, and in the best hours we ever had on earth in the most countenanced public ordinances, or in the sweetest secret duties of His worship.

Nay, which is yet more, there we shall serve Him as well as ever He commanded us to serve Him, or shall desire us to serve Him. We surely will be in such a spiritually noble state as we never before served Him while we sojourned here on earth. Alas! How few, how very few, how lamentably few, are there, even among the great multitudes of professing Christians, of pretenders to godliness, and to the hope of that gain and blessedness which attends them who die in the Lord, who make it the great business of their life to live thus: even all the days of their appointed time to wait till their change comes, coveting and crying in prayer to God that He would graciously and effectually so teach them to number their days that they may apply their hearts to wisdom?

The story is told of one Similis, captain of the Roman emperor Hadrian's guard, who had lived long in the city and at court, and had some seven years before his death retired to a private country house, where he thought that he enjoyed himself more, being freed from the avocations, distractions, noise, and cumbersome converse of a court life. He commanded that after his death it should be written over his grave, "Here lies Similis who was many years old, but lived only seven." How many professors of religion are there, I say, who may thus sadly and sorrowfully complain of themselves when they come to die, "Ah! we have been here many years, but have lived either none at all, or but very few years." For that life that is not lived to God, and to the honor and glory of Jesus Christ, is not at all worthy of the denomination of "life," since we are, all the time we live so, but dead while we live.

It is astonishing to think that reasonable men and women—professing to have immortal souls, living especially under the clear light and sunshine of the gospel, who do not at all design nor endeavor to live to God, nor to live the life that they now live in the flesh by the faith of the Son of God—should foolishly fancy themselves to live, and fondly flatter themselves in a golden dream that they shall be well at death, die in the Lord, and so be blessed with them who die thus; who rest from their labors, and whose works follow them; who enter into peace and rest in their beds, every one walking in his uprightness. Oh, fool's paradise! Oh, deplorable and damnable delusion! Whoever therefore would be (as all of us are unspeakably concerned to be) undeceived as to this self-murdering and soul-ruining gross, practical error and mistake, and who seriously and sincerely desire to live so as to have the well-grounded hope of dying in the Lord, and of being truly blessed at and after their death (without which it had been much better for them never to have lived at all, or to have lived the life of brutes, even of the most abject, vile, contemptible, and abominable brutes, which when they are dead are done, annihilated, and gone), let them diligently peruse and gravely ponder these few following sermons, and pray for the blessing of them. The design (excellently driven by the author, who most edifying and exemplarily, most convincingly and comfortably live and die thus) is to rectify such miserable mistakes, and to air right (which he does by a most admirably divine art) towards the only sure and safe way of dying happily, which is by living holily.

Christian reader, you may have read several other tracts on this subject, but I suppose you have hardly read any more solidly and succinctly, more pertinently, powerfully, and pungently written, and, withal, more suited to the various cases and conditions of all sorts of readers than this. As for me, while I was revising these sermons and making them ready for the press, I was sometimes, as I still am, made to doubt (I shall not deny but my little acquaintance with other men's writings may considerably influence this doubt) whether any ordinary minister of the gospel has readily handled so many notable purposes to better purpose, several of them surprising, yet all of them clearly dependent upon, and natively consequent unto, one another in so few words.

Read then this little book (which is Mr. Durham's, from whose pen or mouth nothing has hitherto dropped into the press that has been unsavory or unacceptable to the churches of Christ) again and again. Digest it well, and I think I may with humble boldness say that if you should read nothing else on this subject but this book, and what is written thereof in the book of the sacred Scriptures (which in this and all the other purposes treated of in it infinitely transcends all the writings of the most able and holy men in the world), you may, through God's blessing, be sufficiently instructed how to die the blessed death of them who die in the Lord.

Now blessed eternally be our blessed Lord Jesus, who by His accursed but most blessed death has procured all this blessedness that attends and follows the death of them who die in Him; who are all blessed, and shall be blessed in despite of the devil, the world, and the remainder of corruption dwelling in them till their dying day. He Himself has pronounced the blessing on them, and who shall dare, who can reverse it? They are all blessed who live and die in the Lord, and none but they. All true blessedness is entailed upon, engrossed and monopolized unto, this honorable society. Not a dram of blessedness is to be found in all the world over, whatever ignorant, deluded, and foolish men may fancy to the contrary. That you may be found associated with this blessed company is the earnest desire of your servant in the gospel,

John Carstairs

1
Death Is Certain

"And I heard a voice from heaven saying unto me, 'Write, blessed are the dead which die in the Lord from henceforth; yea,' saith the Spirit, 'that they may rest from their labors; and their works do follow them.'"

Revelation 14:13

These words are singularly useful, material, and momentous in themselves; and it is not for naught that the Spirit of God puts such a mark on them, and that a special commission is given to John to write them. We have therefore thought it meet to speak a word of them beyond what we can easily teach in the lecture, since they include a truth of such great concern to us regarding the right way of dying and the happiness that follows them that die in the Lord. Blessedness has in all ages been thought of and sought after by men, though alas many have sadly mistaken it, and the way how to come at it, here is the nearest step and door to it, even to die rightly and well, and that is to die in the Lord.

That we may open up the meaning of the words a little, we would consider that this verse, set down by way of transition, couples the two last parts of the chapter together; for when John has spoken of the warning and advertisement given to the world by the ministers of the gospel, ere he comes to denounce judgment for despising the preached gospel, these sweet words are interjected by a voice from heaven. "Write," says He, "blessed are the dead which die in the Lord."

The scope of them then is this: since there were sad

and doleful days coming, and judgments were likely to be very universal after God begins to reckon for despising the gospel, so that He may both set out the greatness and terribleness of the judgments and comfort the godly against them, the Lord bids John write down that none who die in Him need to be afraid of them. It is as if He had said, "Though these judgments that are coming will be very great, though many will be removed and swept away by them, and though withal the coming calamities will be such that the godly will be ready to think them happy who were taken away, yet, notwithstanding, all these who die in Me are blessed."

There are four things to consider in this verse:

1. A preface: "I heard a voice from heaven, saying unto me, 'Write,' " importing the weightiness of the matter and commission; for it is sent from heaven to John and he is bidden write it. It is a heavenly message sent by Christ to His Church, and even to His Church in these times and days wherein we live.

2. A plain maxim, conclusion, or general doctrine laid down as a most certain truth: "Write, says He, 'Blessed are the dead which die in the Lord.' " "Register and record this," says Christ. It has been and shall be a most infallible certain truth to the end of the world, let never so many conclusions come, and let kingdoms be turned upside down: "They are blessed who die in Me."

3. There is a qualification of this truth not denying the universality of it, but seeming to apply it as especially verified in such a time from henceforth: "Yea, saith the Spirit."

We cannot so expound these words, as if the meaning of them were that from the time of their death they are blessed who die in the Lord, though that is a truth, because, first, it does not agree with the scope. These words are a diversion relating to this time, and intended for a peculiar comfort to the godly against the evils of judgment coming in this time. Second, it will not agree with the practice here used, "from henceforth" or "now" (as it is in the original) to expound it so, for then it would have been said, "from thenceforth," that is, from their death forward. But it is "from henceforth," that is, now, in this sad time that is coming. And if any should ask what shall be the singular happiness that these shall have who, after this time, shall die in the Lord, the answer may be drawn from the reason that is subjoined, which is the fourth thing in the text.

4. The reason: that they may rest from their labors, and their works do follow them. This implies a special tossing and troublesome time coming, and says that it is very good to be in heaven ere that time comes. Out of this reason we may see a threefold respect wherein the happiness of those who die in the Lord is applicable to this time, and they all agree to the scope:

(1) They are freed from much tossing toil and trouble that the surviving godly would be involved in, who should have a hard and toilsome life of it under the coming judgments (for the scope is to set out the greatness of the approaching judgments). And they are happy who are taken away from the evil to come, as Solomon says in Ecclesiastes 4:2: "I praised the dead which are already dead, more than the living which are yet alive," meaning they are freed from these troubles, vanities, and vexations that the living were weighted down with. They are freed from a toilsome and troublesome world, more so now and at this time than at other times.

(2) They are happy that now, when the gospel has broken out, they die with more confidence, being freed from the fear of purgatory, being clear in the matter of their salvation, and assured of their going

immediately to paradise. This is held forth in the end
of the words, in that it is said "their works do follow
them." Though they have no expectation of receiving
anything by way of merit, yet it shall be well with them
who have kept a good conscience, for they shall eat the
fruit of their doings, as it is in Isaiah 3:10; for though
God does not give anything to His people for their
works, yet He rewards them according to their works, so
proportioning His proceeding with them as nothing
shall be found to have been done by them for Him for
naught. It is a special part of their happiness that they
shall be freed from the anxiety that the darkness of
these superstitious times kept men under, being now
cleared by the light of the gospel.

(3) Comparing this with verse 11, they are
blessed who die now in the Lord after life and immortality are brought to light by the gospel because they
are freed from the scorching hell that these got who
worshipped the beast. Now when the light has come,
are they not blessed who die in the Lord and are freed
from that which they would have met with if they had
not lived and died in Him, but in darkness and ignorance of Him? And so the words say that when the
gospel breaks forth, men must resolve to live and die in
Christ, or to live and die in a most damnable condition
than the heavens that lived before them without the
gospel.

In this conclusion or general doctrine we have
these three things employed:

First, something common to all, and that is dying.
Good and bad all must die.

Second, there is a difference in dying to some,
though death is common to all, and that is to die in the
Lord.

Third, there is a peculiar effect or advantage to
them who die with this qualification, and that is hap-

piness or blessedness; and these two imply that there are many who do not die in the Lord, and that consequently they are accursed who neither live nor die in Him.

The general doctrine is plain, and it greatly concerns every one to take notice of it. It would be good if this text were engraved in deep and legible characters on our hearts so that we may learn to reckon blessedness not so much from our life as from our living and dying jointly together. Be what we will in our life, if we do not die in Christ, there is a great flaw in our happiness, a curse instead of a blessing; and if this indispensably requisite qualification is in it, it entitles us to this blessedness. Oh, therefore, let these plain words, and the necessity of the doctrine, speak to you.

First, there is a necessity of dying lying on all, for it says plainly that there is a dying that is in the Lord and a dying that is out of the Lord, and all sorts of men and women die in one of these ways. It is as if He has said, "Would you know who are indeed happy? It is not all who die, but such only as die in the Lord." You know what death is, I do not need to describe it to you; and you are disposed to think that it does not need to be proved that all must die. I wish it needed no proof; however, see Hebrews 9:27 ("It is appointed to men once to die") and Romans 5:12 and 14, where it is said that death hath passed upon all men, and that death reigns over all men. Death is certain from its cause, which is sin, and God's curse on sin, that death is the wages of sin; and where sin is the cause, death must be the effect. Yea, it may be confirmed from nearly 6000 years experience, wherein all who have been born throughout all generations have died.

I do not speak of the extraordinary examples of Enoch and Elijah, who were particularly and singularly by the sovereign dominion of God exempted from death. Neither will I speak of what the Lord did to them in place of death, or for putting them in a capacity to sustain immortality. God's ordinary way of dealing with men is that which we are called to look to; it is enough that they have put off mortality and put on immortality, though we do not know the manner and way. Simply look on the race of mankind and you will find that these who lived longest died at last, as did Adam, Enos, Cain, Mahalaleel, Jared, and Methuselah, who, though he lived 969 years, yet died. It is said in Ecclesiastes 8:8, "There is no man that hath power over the spirit to retain it, neither hath he power in the day of death: and there is no discharge in that war, neither shall wickedness deliver those that are given to it." There is no man who has power to keep his soul in his body; there is no demission or furlough in that war, no way to escape death. The most profane man who puts death furthest off from him shall not escape it; and seeing he takes it for granted, and all generations have proved the truth of it, I shall insist no further on the proof of it, but come to the use.

USE 1. This doctrine serves to settle and fix the impression of the truth of this point deeply upon us, and withal to reprove our living so much from under and without it. Alas, we ordinarily take general truths for granted, but as for any suitable use or application of them in our practice we live for most part as if they were untruths. We live as mortal in respect of sickness, infirmities, and fears, but we live as immortal in respect of the stayed thoughts of a world to come.

Let me therefore pose a question to you in sober sadness: how often do you think seriously about dying? When did you lay your reckoning solidly for it? When did you descend into your hearts to see how it would be with you at death? How often have you made your testament this way to say so? And when did you take your leave and say farewell to the things of a world and lay them some way by on the consideration that death will make a final separation between you and them?

Take these evidences that you do not indeed mind death and mortality:

First, the stupid security we generally live under, and our great unwatchfulness, says plainly that we do not really regard death; if we were thinking on death would we not be so careless in counting with God and so little afraid what will become of the immortal soul, and live as if there were not a life eternal. We would not be as those of the old world did who ate and drank and never once altered their pace. Ah! Is it not so with most people now? Death lights unaware, like a falcon out of the air on most men because this general truth is not practically believed. There could not be such deep and senseless security if there were serious thoughts and real belief of dying.

Second, the great earthly-mindedness and insatiable coveting and lusting after the things of the world, as if men were perpetually to abide with them, clearly and convincingly speak of this truth. Believe me, serious thoughts of dying would greatly wean and estrange men from these things. Men, alas, seek after a happiness here in time as if they were to have an eternal abode in the world, as that poor rich man in the gospel did who brutishly said to his soul, "Soul, take thy rest, for thou hast much good laid up for many years; eat and drink and be merry" (Luke 12:19). If men were looking for death, surely they would not thus glut themselves with these worldly empty things—huge, disproportioned objects to satisfy the vast appetite of an immortal soul which, by its constitution, is elevated to the capacity of a happiness of a higher and more excellent nature than these things can possibly amount unto. Take this, then, for palpable evidence of your atheism and unbelief in this important point, and let the thoughts of death come in to bound and moderate your eager and inordinate pursuit of the world.

Third, the great and intolerable pride and loftiness of men and women is a demonstration of this. If you minded death in good earnest, and believed that it were near even at the door, and that your last breath is in your nostrils, it would make you humble in your walking with God and in your conversing one with another.

Fourth, there is such little preparation for dying and for the life to come, as if there were no more, says plainly and undeniably that you do not lay death seriously to heart. If you did, you would be seeking more to lay up treasures in heaven and to be flitting (to say so) your affections there, and towards things above, and to be casting your anchor within the veil.

USE 2. In opposition to the former security and stupid unconcernedness, let me beseech you to mind this more seriously, which is so certain, and to take more pains to prepare yourselves for it. Eternity is long, oh, vastly and incomprehensibly long; heaven and hell are matters of unspeakably great moment and consequence. When the master or good man of the house has laid down and shut the door, there will thenceforth be no opening of it. It is now your summer, so provide for your long winter. It is bad stewardship to put off that which is of greatest concern, and to put off securing your eternal state till the time of sickness and death. You do not know if you ever shall get relief from any lengthened disease; neither do you know but that you may be snatched away in a moment all of a sudden. Believe this: it is no common thing to die well, and to have death as the entry and door to happiness.

Therefore, to stir you up seriously and immediately to mind dying so that you may not say with the sluggard, "Yet a little sleep, yet a little slumber, and yet a little folding of the hands to sleep," whereby the fool is slain, consider these things:

1. It will not be bare wishes that will make you die well. Balaam had many such wishes to die the death of the righteous, and yet was none the better for them. Do not spend not your days idly; do not trifle away your time unprofitably, for death is always coming on, and will not wait for you to prepare before it comes. Seek therefore to be found in a watchful and praying frame, for blessed is that servant who, when his master comes, is found in that posture waiting for the coming of his Lord and ready to open to Him immediately (or at the very first knock) as it is in Luke 12:36. Oh, strangely emphatic word!

2. Consider how few they are who at death are ready, and how few they are who at death get the liberty and blessing to make themselves ready. I grant that one thief on the cross finds mercy so that none may despair, yet it is but one so that none may presume; but that all may be alarmed to look well and watchfully to themselves, many will go to hell, no doubt, who will seek to enter into heaven and yet will not be able. A sort of whining and yowling at death may be in very godless and atheistic persons because they did not begin in time to seek to enter, as the scope of that parable shows. If you could just hear the language of many in hell, how they would preach this point! Beware of dallying and putting off the time; many who are in hell, if you could hear them speak, would readily say, "Oh, that was our ruin, and undid us!" But if the Word of God does not affect you, nor work you up to the serious consideration of this, though one should rise from the dead and preach to you, it would not affect you to any advantage.

3. Consider that the longer you think on death, the less terrible it will be when it comes. Serious and suit-

able thoughts of death beforehand would do much to mitigate the terror of it, but when death comes violently and suddenly on you, and finds you settled in the world, in that case indeed it will come as the king of terrors; whereas if you were dying daily, and by conversing with death came to have experience as it were of little deaths beforehand, that would make death itself when it should come much more easy. Especially would this be so if you were dying to your lusts and idols, were mortified to the world and to the things that are in it, then death would have in that case little to do when it came; for it is the cleaving of your hearts to these things, and your being glued to them, that makes death so terrible, for it will not try nor treat, but suddenly and inexorably separate you and them.

4. Consider that the longer you put off thinking of your eternal state, and thinking seriously of dying, the more you will have to do when death comes. Oh, there is much work about dying, even to these who have been thinking on it, how to get faith in Christ right, how to get themselves rolled on the everlasting covenant of salvation, how to be in a patient calm and composed frame to encounter the terror that accompanies death, how to be weaned from the world and to have their affections heavenly. Surely, the longer you put it off, the more you will have to do, and will readily be less able to do it. Is it wisdom, do you think, to leave your greatest and most necessary work to your last, weakest, and most unfit time to go about it? Yet, alas, this is the lamentable, foolish, demented, rueful, and soul-ruining practice even of many hearers of the gospel; there is none of these things but it must be done before death or not at all. What is in the bargain or business then? Oh, what is in it? It's not ten or twenty thousand years' happiness or misery, but an eternity of happiness or misery in the greatest measure and highest degree that

can be imagined! And should such a business be delayed and put off? This is even that in the text by which dying in the Lord is so much commended.

Now before I close this sermon, let me speak a word regarding what it is to die in the Lord, which is held forth as the great and necessary qualification of them who die with well-grounded confidence, and who warrantably expect happiness. There are three Scripture phrases that are very conducive to the opening of it:

1. It implies being in Christ, as that word is in 2 Corinthians 5:17: "If any man be in Christ, he is a new creature." This holds out our union with Him by faith, when Christ opens His arms and takes the soul in to Himself which flies to Him, closes with and cleaves to Him. This is the first step and ground of happiness, and it has with it a new nature and a new life.

2. The second phrase is found in Galatians 2:20: "I live, yet not I, but Christ liveth in me, and the life that I now live in the flesh I live by the faith of the Son of God." This is a step further, when a man by faith has fled to Christ, and improves and makes use of His title to Him and interest in Him so as to perform the acts of life. Living in Christ or by the faith of Christ expresses and holds forth a new nature and life in the acts of life in bringing forth the fruits of the Spirit, and makes the person indeed a Christian man or man-Christian, doing not only the duties of religion, but all his moral, civil, and natural actions to Christ, living thus Christian-like, as spiritual and from the Spirit, living not to ourselves but to Him.

3. There is a dying in the Lord here in the text which follows upon the former. Living in Him is the way to happiness, and dying in Him is the very door through which a man enters into the profession of happiness. Now this dying in the Lord presupposes the former, and has something more in it, to wit, as an act-

ing of faith for living in Him, so an acting of faith for dying in Him. It takes in:

• Fleeing to Christ afresh and anew for refuge, as it is in Philippians 3:9. It is seeking to be found in Him, leaping as it were out of ourselves and taking ourselves to Him as our ship to sail in through death to life, renouncing our own righteousness anew and closing with His; yea, and renouncing the very acts of our faith such as they are.

• It takes in a giving of credit to Christ for bearing us through death, acquiescing in and resting on Him on that ground, sticking close by Him, being well content and satisfied to adventure to go through death in His hand, and having gotten a word from Christ resolvedly to keep the grip of it. With old Simeon we can now say, "Let Thy servant depart in peace. Lord, I am content to take shipping, as it were, in Christ, and in that bottom to sail through the gulf of death when Thou willest."

• It takes in a humble quieting and satisfying of ourselves on this ground, not only delighting ourselves in Him as all-sufficient, but comforting ourselves in our thus resting on Him, and counting ourselves happy in it. Something of all these last three we will find held forth in the so-called last words of David, his swan-like song when he is going to die, found in 2 Samuel 23:5: "Although my house be not so with God, yet He hath made with me an everlasting covenant."

David takes himself and flees for his life to the grace of God in Christ, held out in the covenant.

David goes forward, trusting himself to and contenting himself in this covenant, calling it a well-ordered and sure covenant, able and sufficient to do his turn. Oh, it is a tight vessel that cannot have a leak! It is as if he had said, "I may sail through death in it safely and not fear."

David delights and satisfies himself in it; he acqui-
esces to it: "This is all my salvation and all my desire. It
is all my heart can wish, it is the very outmost measure
of my wishes. I need no more and I desire no more."

Now when I speak of dying in the Lord, I would have
you take all three steps together. First, study to be in
Him. There is no possible dying in Him without being
in Him; any who would be happy by dying in Him
would by all means accept the offer of the gospel. Flee
to Christ for refuge, close with Him by faith, and endeavor to put it out of question that you are in Him. Oh,
make sure that you have given Him a soul to save, and
acquiesce in Him as your Savior.

Second, live by faith in Him. None can expect to die
in Christ who never seriously sought to live in Him.
Make it manifest that you live in Him by having another sort of life than brutish men have who are still in
their natural state. God may call a thief on the cross
and make him die in Christ who has not lived in Him,
but none of you can comfortably expect that He will
deal so with you. And where one is so dealt with, twenty,
if not a hundred, even very many, die without it.

And let me say this, if ever at anytime God was striking men and women with stupidity at death, it is palpable He is striking many so in this time. It may be that
some of you know that God is striking some with stupidity who made a mockery of the serious exercise of
godliness in their lifetime. Therefore I say again, make
your being in Christ sure; evidence your being in Him
by your living in Him and to Him. I shall not insist further at this time on this subject. God calls us all seriously to think on it. Sickness, smiting with judgments,
and death have not readily been more frequent; and if
ever there was a time when folk were called to believe
and lay to heart such a doctrine, this is the time. There
may be some here who ere a few days go by may experi-

ence the truth of it, and who knows who these some shall be? As you expect happiness, learn to die, and as to die in Christ so to live in Him; and as the Lord bids John write these words, so I bid you read them and think often on them: "Blessed are the dead that die in the Lord from henceforth, that they may rest from their labors, and their works do follow them."

2

The Way to True Blessedness

"Blessed are the dead which die in the Lord."
Revelation 14:13

There is one thing common to all men, and that is
a natural inclination to, and an appetite and desire after, happiness or blessedness. But there are two things
wherein the most men exceedingly err: (1) in seeking
blessedness where it is not to be found, and in accounting that to be blessedness which is not so, but leaves
them eternally miserable; (2) that when some glances
of happiness and wherein it consists are gotten, they
grossly mistake the way to come by it. The words of our
text give a notable description of true blessedness, and
a clear direction towards the way how to come at it.
They show plainly where it lies, let the blind and preju-
diced world esteem it as they will: "blessed are the dead
which die in the Lord." That is only true blessedness
which the dead in the Lord enjoy, and that's the only
way to true blessedness: to be in Christ and to live and
die in Him. This is a most concerning subject, and singularly suitable to our times.

The doctrine which we shall now propose and prosecute lies plainly and obviously in the very words of the
text: they are blessed and happy, yea, they only are
blessed and happy, who are dead in the Lord Christ or
shall die in Him. A voice from heaven asserts it to John,
and the Spirit adds a confirmation of it, the Spirit of
Christ and the Spirit of truth.

15

Before I proceed further, I shall in a word or two clear these things in the doctrines which are also in the words.

1. What is this blessedness? It is spoken of here as that which is singularly so; it's the only happy condition that can be truly thought of in all the world; it's even to be fully and completely blessed.

2. What is the necessary qualification of these persons who are pronounced to be blessed? It's not those who die, but those who die in the Lord that are thus blessed. To clear this beside what I said the last day, I shall now add that there are two sorts of dying spoken of in Scripture. First, there is a dying in sin. "If ye believe not in Me, ye shall die in your sins," said Christ to the Jews in John 8:24. And this implies two things: One, you shall die under the guilt of your sins, and under the curse and wrath of God, which you deserve, before death, at death, and after death. Two, you shall die in a sinful estate in opposition to repentance for sin; you shall slip away and be removed in that sinful condition; you shall depart and go off the world in that sinful state. Oh, what a sad and sorrowful departure!

Second, there is a dying in the Lord, and this implies two things also as opposed to dying in sin: One, that persons in the sense of their sin have taken themselves to Christ and are freed from the guilt of sin by faith in Him, and are clothed with His righteousness, or with a right and title to it. Two, it implies a breaking off of the course of sin, and bringing forth the fruits of a new nature and life by a lively faith in Christ in whom, as the true vine, they are as so many branches grafted abiding in Him and bringing forth fruit to Him so that His Father may be glorified and they manifested to be His disciples (John 15); who, as they have union with Him by faith, so they have communion with Him in the fruits of sanctification. These and these only are thus blessed, and this blessedness is restricted unto and entailed upon them only, and peremptorily denied to all others, and they utterly excluded from it.

In prosecuting the doctrine I shall, first, clear the truth of this, that they are blessed, exceedingly blessed and only blessed, who are dead or shall die in the Lord. Second, I shall offer reasons to prove that this blessedness is peculiar to them and not to any other. Third, I shall speak a little to the use and improvement of it.

They are exceedingly blessed who are dead or shall die in the Lord. We need to do no more but to describe happiness or blessedness, and we will find it exactly to agree in all its properties and circumstances to them who are dead or shall die in Christ. Oh, do not look on this as a story or some airy notion, but as that which is a great reality, a thing which some of our Christian acquaintances who are dead in the Lord now enjoy, and which others ere long shall enjoy, and that which by faith in Him you may all enjoy. There are two things necessary to, and constitutive of, true blessedness or happiness. The first is an absolute freedom from all evil, from every thing that troubles or may be the cause of trouble, and from any sinful blamable or unsuitable defect or want; for happiness cannot consist or stand with anything of that kind. The second is a concurrence of all the good things that are necessary to complete blessedness or happiness, both of which are enjoyed by all those who die in the Lord, and by them only.

They who die in the Lord are perfectly freed from all evil, which holds true whether we look to it more generally, or with more particular respect to the scope. They are freed from all those evils that an evil time brings with it. To descend into the particular consideration of this blessedness would not be easy; let us only therefore look on some general headings to clear it so far forth as concerns the present point.

They have freedom from all sin, that is the fountain of all evils. The spirits of just men are made perfect; no corrupt flesh or blood is permitted to come before the throne; no rebellion in the law of the members or against the law of the mind is there. There is no remainder of the evil heart of unbelief in drawing aback from the living God, nor any wearying of holy duties, but only a delightful serving of God day and night, that is, without any the least interruption; for there is no day and night, but constant day in that life.

Then that petition which is so often put up to Him in His peoples' prayers ("Thy will be done . . . as it is in heaven") is fulfilled; there is then a most perfect doing of His will; there His servants serve Him in such a spiritually noble state as He was never served by them on earth. This light, vain, and unstable heart shall then be established and fixed as an immovable pillar in the temple of God. The looseness of a wavering, gauding, and wandering mind shall then be quite and forever removed, and the thoughts of it so strongly stayed in the contemplation of that most blessed Object that they shall not for so much as one moment be diverted. There will not then be the least inclination to nor capacity of a diversion. Oh, what would some of us give (could it be bought) for this kind of happiness, to be fully and finally delivered from a body of death, from the many sinful pranks of it, and the dangerous precipices it drives them upon?

Next, they have perfect freedom from all temptations to sin. There does not in that most clear and serene upper region breathe the least air of temptation; there is no temptation to sin from without as there is no inclination to sin from within, and consequently there is a full freedom from all fear of hazard and danger of sinning. No unclean thing comes within the gates of the new Jerusalem since sin, death, and the devil have been cast into the lake of fire. There is no evil example there, but, on the contrary, if there were any need of stirring up, strengthening, and encouraging one another, it is there eminently. There is withal a holy freedom from the difficulty that is in watching here, which, though it is a useful and necessary duty in sojourning saints, yet it has with it a painfulness and fear, from which the triumphing saints who are dead in the Lord are perfectly freed.

They are freed from all challenges for sin; they have there no troublesome nor disquieting exercise of conscience. The immediate enjoyment of God's company so quiets and satisfies them that nothing can disquiet them. There they are under no desertion or fear of desertion. There are often two sad exercises to the godly here: the challenges of their conscience for sin, and the weight on their spirits because of desertion. There is moreover no lukewarm or lifeless spiritual condition there, but a condition that is always fresh, lively, and at the very best. They are continually praising in the sense of the love of God overflowing them in duty. The dead in the Lord must then certainly be in a most happy condition when they are freed from all these, and from all fear of them.

They are freed from all the effects of sin. There is no curse, no wrath, no sickness of body, no anxiety of mind there, no terror nor apprehension of indignation, no poverty, no scarcity or want to them of anything there (however poor a life they may have here)— but God is all and in all, He by Himself immediately fills the place of all things, and fills up the vastest capacities of the soul.

They are also freed from all the tossings and troubles that are here in this lower world. There are no confinings or refinings, no sequestrations or forfeitures or hazard of losing estates, no quarterings of soldiers to discompose the quiet and tranquility of families there, which some would think a piece of happiness to be rid of. There is no reproach, no discredit or disgrace there, but a new name given. There are no mistakes or jealousies, no alienations or animosities, no rents or divisions, no unsuitable passions or heats there, but a most comely and complete union and holy harmony in praising God. There is no darkness of mind there, the understanding being perfectly enlightened; no disorder in the affections, but a most exact regularity; no perverseness or backwardness in the will, but a most thorough compliance in all things with the will of God, all within the man, sweetly conspiring in a holy harmony and in due subordination to the head. There is no scandal or offense given or taken there. There are no sad reports or ill news there; nay, it's impossible there can be since God orders all immediately; and they approve all that He does. They applaud and are well satisfied with all. There are no overturnings of kingdoms and states, nor confusions or desolations in churches to mar their happiness there; but they are fully acquainted with the infinitely wise proceedings of God. There is nothing that can mar their happiness. Suppose they knew all these overturnings, confusions and distractions that make us sad here below; they cannot be troubled with the want (or with the fear of the want) of anything—and thus they continue to be forever and ever. Yet this is but a little piece of their happiness who die in the Lord. How small a portion of it we know!

As to the other half of their happiness (and, oh, that you would know and believe what the happiness is which they have who are now before the throne), there is in it a concurrence of all good things necessary for making them completely happy; and it must have these four things concurring to this end, which are all in their estate who die in the Lord: First, there is an enjoying of God as the chief good, for no other thing or person can communicate true happiness, nor make one truly happy. Second, because there cannot be any enjoying of Him without some suitableness to Him, therefore a suitableness for the enjoyment of God is required; for we could not, we ought not fully and immediately enjoy God in the estate wherein we now are. Third, it requires full measures and degrees of enjoying God. Fourth, it requires a perpetual and eternal enjoying of Him, and all these concur, as I said, to complete the happiness of them that die in the Lord.

1. They fully enjoy God as the chief good. Where Abraham is, there are they; he is in the kingdom of his Father, and so are they, and therefore are most happy. Hence it is that Christ, speaking of blessedness to His disciples, tells them that they shall sit with Abraham, Isaac, and Jacob in the kingdom of heaven (Matthew 8:11). They have places among them who stand by (Zechariah 3:7); they see His face and are therefore happy, since "blessed are the pure in heart, for they shall see God" (Matthew 5:8). When we speak of enjoying God, it is far, very far above and beyond what we can express. It must surely be a great happiness and delight when the object of their delight is no created thing, but the infinite and all-sufficient God; it must be a pure heavenly and excellent delight that flows from the enjoyment of God, with whom is the fountain of life.

2. They are made fit and suitable to enjoy Him in a full measure and in a high degree. If we could imagine man's understanding to be enlarged so as to conceive of God, and the enlargement of it to be very far beyond that which we can now imagine or conceive, it shall be thus dilated and filled; it shall then have a distinct and fully satisfying knowledge of the great mystery of the

adorable Trinity, as Christ assures His disciples in John 14:20: "At that day ye shall know that I am in the Father." The affections shall then be made capacious to receive, and shall be filled and satisfied with delight in the enjoyment of that clearly and distinctly known object. It satisfies angels, and must satisfy the spirits of just men made perfect; it makes them happy to behold and enjoy Him, and the greatest happiness that the Scripture speaks of is to be in Christ's company, beholding the glory that He has gotten from the Father.

If you could suitably conceive what condition David, Paul, and some who have gone a few years or months since into that blessed rest are in, it would make you long to die in the Lord, and would through grace put you to give all diligence in time to make that happiness sure.

3. As they are made suitable and meet to enjoy God in a full measure and high degree, so they shall enjoy Him in a full measure and degree actually. There is no more desired nor desirable; it is full glory and full joy. None can imagine or wish more, it being a thing to which there can be no accession made according to the capacity that they are put into; for though there are different degrees of glory, and some conceive and receive more and some less, yet all are filled even filled with the love and lovingkindness of God, with that fullness of joys and those pleasures that are at His right hand. And they have all this not in bare notions, but most really and in an incomprehensible way (to us now, at least, incomprehensible) communicated to them.

4. This enjoying of God is perpetual and eternal, forever and ever without interruption or intermission. It is not only a full, but an everlasting joy and glory. Sorrow and sighing shall then forever flee away, and everlasting joy shall be upon their heads forevermore.

The crown is an eternal and imperishable one, even a crown of life that is perpetually flourishing. Yet all that we have said falls hugely short of it and is, as to our manner of expressing it, unworthy to be compared with the happiness of them who die in the Lord. If any of them heard us speak of their condition, they would wonder to hear us do it so childishly, poorly, meanly, and weakly. Oh, that we could stretch ourselves to believe that which we cannot so distinctly conceive of this blessedness!

The next thing I proposed to speak a word or two to is the reasons why blessedness is peculiar only to them who die in the Lord, and not to any others. I shall shortly hint at three:

First, only they who die in the Lord Christ are made partakers of His satisfaction, and therefore they and they only are freed from the curse by believing in Him (John 3:36). "He that believeth on Him is not condemned, but hath everlasting life; but he that believeth not is condemned already and the wrath of God abideth on him" (John 3:18 and 36). They who believe have gotten a discharge of their debt, and the handwriting that was against them is cancelled. But they that believe not have the bond still standing over their heads, and for their undischarged debt shall be hauled before the Judge and cast in prison, where they must lie till they pay the utmost farthing, which will never be done.

Second, only they who are in Christ and die in Him are privileged with the adoption of sons, and consequently only they only have a right to heaven and eternal life. "To as many as received Him gave He power to become the sons of God," that is, "to as many as believed on His name" (John 1:12). "And if sons, then heirs, and joint heirs with Christ" (Romans 8:17). If we are not sons, then are we not heirs.

Third, only they who live and die in Christ are new creatures. "If any man be in Christ Jesus, he is a new creature" (2 Corinthians 5:17). "And in Christ Jesus, nothing avails but a new creature" (Galatians 6:15). "Except a man be born again, he cannot enter into the kingdom of heaven" (John 3:3). And there being none born again but they who are in Christ, and our regeneration and faith in Christ going inseparably together, none can be happy but those who live and die in Him.

Application

I come now to the uses of this doctrine, which must be many, being such a high point as holds forth the right way and the only way to true blessedness.

USE 1. Let this doctrine put us all to be more seriously exercised how to die well, and that is to die in the Lord. Seeing that such a happiness depends on it, and only on it, then surely folks should be exceedingly concerned to walk by this course of dying in Him if they would meet with happiness at the end. There are many things that press this.

• If peace and tranquility of mind and conscience are of concern, then this is of concern; for how can they possibly have peace who do not know whether they shall go to heaven or hell?

• If comfort in anything or all things is of concern, then this is of concern; for how can men's sleep, meat, drink, apparel, or anything that they enjoy, be comfortable to them if they do not know that they are in Him and shall die in Him? This one word may mar all their mirth and happiness, that they who are not in Him shall die miserably and so lose all other comforts.

• If it is of concern to have boldness and confidence towards God at death, this is of concern; for if death sadly surprises men, how can they have peace, confidence, or boldness since they are not in Him? All the world cannot buy or purchase a quiet and good conscience for them.

• If we think heaven or happiness to be of concern, then this is no doubt of concern; for heaven and happiness are knit to dying in Him. Therefore let me in the name of the Lord lay it upon you, by all suitable means, to endeavor to bear it upon your very hearts to have your peace with God made in time so that, die when you will, it may be made sure that your death shall be in Him. Do you think that to be eternally in heaven or in hell is of little concern? It is your way of dying that makes the difference. As the tree falls, so it will lie; there will be no revoking of that sentence, nor any change of your state after death—and do any of you know when it will come? Are any sure to get time or grace then to make peace with God when sickness and death comes? Are there not many stricken with hardness, senselessness, and conscience-numbing stupidity at their death? Remember therefore that death is coming, and study to have this much in your eye.

This use serves to reprove the great stupidity that most live in, as if they did not care how they die. For how many grossly profane and atheistic men live as if they were to die like beasts? And how many presumptuous hypocrites are there who think it is a very easy matter to die, yea, that it is nothing? How many are there who have frequent fears and convictions, especially at death, who yet never come this length to make it sure on good grounds that their sins are laid on Christ, and to make it their great business to have their corruption mortified by His grace so that they may die in Him? How many are there who have some good in them, who are very lazy and careless, and who in a manner let death come as it will? I shall (seeing it is of such mighty concern) press it on you by laying before you some things that are very ordinary to men and women at death.

We look alas upon death afar off, but we should bring it near to us and have it always before us, the neglect whereof makes folk very ordinarily to die as they live, and that is neither well nor in the Lord. There are four cases or conditions that we most ordinarily meet with in the plurality of them who die.

First, we find some senseless and stupid, without any fear of God or regard for their souls. They lived a stupid life without any fear and awe of the majesty of God, and they die just so. Thus churlish Nabal died as he lived, most stupidly and senselessly. It might possibly be edifying, though very sad, to speak of the lamentable condition of some graceless persons who die among us; therefore put away senselessness and stupidity now along your life if you would not die senseless and stupid.

A second sort of persons we meet with are those who have been presuming all their days and must pertinaciously dispute it out at their death that all shall be well with them; and though it may be palpably discerned that they are without all due sense of sin and utterly void of grace, yet they will confidently aver that they believed all their days, and will not quit their deluding hopes that all shall be well with them now at death. O sirs, do you think that you are in a good condition if you die without a sense of sin, and with tasteless, lifeless, and groundless apprehensions of mercy? Dread, therefore, and deprecate presumption. Oh, but it is hard to get some of you convinced of it, and yet it is a special thing that keeps you from coming in good earnest to Christ.

A third sort are these who die with some little challenges, and at best with much doubting and many fears; who have had their own convictions, fears, and doubtings in their life, and yet never labored in God's way to be thorough in the matter of their interest in and peace with God. They are afraid to die, and yet die they must. The faith they had misgives them, and the strong apprehensions they have of wrath quite over-turns their confidence and hope, which is the just rec-ompense of living in a doubtful and doubting condi-tion without serious seeking after thorough clearness. I grant that this condition is somewhat better than any of the former two, and yet it is an evil and dangerous condition to die in. Words spoken to them neither sat-isfy nor settle them, for either they have little judgment, or temptations are strong and vigorous, or bodily in-firmities is growing fast on them.

There is a fourth sort of self-righteous persons who please themselves with a hope of heaven, because they have been good neighbors, and lived harmlessly. They were not grossly profane; they were not drunkards, swearers, Sabbath-breakers, or extortioners, but rather were civil and honest, faithful and just in their dealings and their callings. They had prayer in their families and in secret; they waited on ordinances. And at death they confirm themselves from these grounds that all shall be well.

I do not condemn duties, God forbid, but it is a sad and hazardous case when they are mainly laid weight on and stuck to at death. Such self-justifiers are brought in by the Lord (Luke 13), saying, "Lord, we have eaten and drunken in Thy presence." Yet He sends them away from Him. See how the proud and self-justifying Pharisee on such grounds as these is sent away unjusti-fied in Luke 18. Habituating themselves to these grounds of confidence in their lifetime makes men stick stiffly to them at their death, and keeps them from seeing the absolute necessity of Christ's imputed righteousness, and from fleeing to it for their justification.

USE 2. This use is an exhortation to stir yourselves up from these considerations to think on death more seriously, and how you may die in the Lord. And to this end, I shall propose three questions that you should be ready to answer at death.

QUESTION 1. How will you answer the challenges that death will readily bring along with it, and urge you for a satisfying answer unto? Where there has been a negligent life, there will be many challenges; yea, where there has been a diligent life there will not be challenges wanting, you would see how to prevent or answer these. I shall instance only five of them:

(1) You have stifled many good purposes and resolutions, or suspended the conscientious execution and practice of them. You have delayed and put off from day to day making your peace with God. How will you answer it when conscience begins to reflect and look back, and to ask how all is? "Is your house out of order through your negligence? Tell me, man, what is the reason you did not make your peace with God sure before this time? Did you shuffle by such and such a duty when you were called to it, and when it was pressed on you? Why did you forbear to mortify such and such a lust?"

Consider, oh, consider how you will answer such a challenge when you will not dare to adventure on death, and yet will not be able to put it off! You secure atheists and condemners of godliness, consider in time what you will say to this.

(2) Conscience will say that you have been busy following some vain lust, busy about enlarging your house, about gathering some gear or riches, about making conquest of such a piece of land. Now what will all these advantage you? And what profit have you of all these things whereof you are now ashamed? Why did

you set your eyes on, why did you bestow so much labor and spend so much time and pains on, that which cannot satisfy, on that which is not? What good will they then do for you? It shall be said to you, "Fool, this night your soul shall be taken from you, and then whose shall these things be?" What advantage is there or can there possibly be in gaining the whole world if you lose your own soul? And, oh, what ground of such challenges are there in this generation? When death comes near to you, this will stick to and gnaw in the consciences of many of you who hear me this day, even that you have been cumbered and careful about many things while, in the meantime, the one thing necessary has been postponed and quite neglected.

(3) A third challenge, the ground whereof is all too common, will be careless, slothful, and idle trifling away and misspending of precious time and neglecting the great work of salvation, letting pass without improvement opportunities of getting good and doing good. You shall look back and ask yourselves, "What have we been doing in our day?" And the conscience will answer and say, "We were vainly discoursing, tippling, vagabonding, and wandering through the fields, busied in doing nothing or worse than nothing." Then you will cry, but in vain, "Oh, to have some of these precious opportunities back again that we thought little of when we had them! We have passed thirty or forty years' time in the world, and yet are no surer of our salvation now than when we came into it. But we have much more sin and guilt than we had." Ah, some will say, "We have lived fifty or sixty years, and yet none of all that time has been well spent."

(4) A fourth challenge will be regarding people's formality and hypocrisy in the worship of God. They came to the church to hear, but slept or wandered, and were not careful to profit; they sat down and prayed, but

were not in earnest in it, they never sought after the Spirit of grace and of supplications. It may be that they prayed in their families and in secret, but when conscience looks back and sees that all has been merely formal and hypocritical work—that they did not know what communion with God was, that they neither knew nor cared to know whether their persons were accepted and their prayers heard, that they did not study experimentally to be acquainted with the life and power of godliness—oh, how sad this will be! And how will it all be answered?

(5) A fifth challenge will be abusing many means of grace, many mercies and favors, such as Sabbaths, sermons, and conferences. You did not live under heathenish or anti-Christian darkness, but where the pure light of the gospel shined clearly. You might have known the right way but would not; you might have made use of such an instrument, of such a sermon, of such fellowship, or of such a book, but did not. And it would have been better with you, but you did not and you would not. Conscience will say, "Here you were negligent; there you dallied; here you wearied, and there you sat up and gave up. And what can you now answer for all this?"

There are many in Glasgow, and elsewhere, who will meet with this challenge, if not with God's judgment, for the sins whereon it is founded. As you would die in the Lord, for Christ's sake, study to prevent such challenges, and to get them scored out by timeous turning to God in Christ, and seriousness in the way of faith and holiness; for assuredly death will bring along with it many more and many other challenges than most have now while they live and are in health. They will prick and bite in another manner than quickly transient lighter touches of convictions do now.

QUESTION 2. How will you answer some peculiar

temptations that death uses to bring along with it? For temptations are then more sly and subtle as challenges are more loud and piercing, and the devil is then more than ordinarily busy; and if temptations are then yielded to, he has almost won the cause. Oh, consider how you will answer these temptations! I shall only instance these five temptations that usually assault and set upon folk at death:

1. The first is a temptation to fret against God's dispensation in removing and calling away a person at such a time and under such circumstances, which fretting flows from an unwillingness to die. Oh, enmity will be ready to burst out in being angry at God's chopping a man down in the midst of such a design and project, or before he got such a bargain ended, such a purchase made, or such a child provided for. And if the devil prevails by this temptation to fret and repine at divine disposal, it will mar the fruit of anything that might be then expected, and will further estrange you from God so that ye cannot come near Him. How rife is such a temptation?

Study to walk therefore in a sweet pliableness and readiness to die, for if you go on following one design after another, and one worldly business after another without this study, you will be taken unaware, suddenly surprised in the midst of them as many are, and be in eminent hazard of being prevailed over by this temptation to fret and grudge at death's arresting, though it is by the great and righteous Judge's order.

2. A second temptation is to atheism. As folk have lived in atheism, so the devil assaults them by temptations to atheism at their death, to make them despise death, and desperately to harden themselves against it, and with a profane and damnable sort of delicacy, like Agag, to throw themselves into the pit. Hence many desperate souls who all their life scoffed at thoughts of

death, so when death comes they do not trouble themselves with it, but shake off all fear and study a sort of godless gallantry of spirit. Seeing that they must die they will die, and will not so much as seem to regard it. But will you outface the wrath of God that way, and dare to laugh in taking the cup of His indignation in your hands? It is true, it is a piece of God's dreadful justice that these who have not stood in awe of Him in their life should die judicially hardened, but such will meet with a most fearful awakening after it.

3. A third temptation is to presumption and hypocrisy, which prevails especially with civil and formal professors. Such presumed and were hypocritical in their life, so the same temptation sticks to them and prevails over them at death. They may speak something of the consolations of God with their mouths when they have no failing of them in their hearts, and of faith in Christ when they never knew the real exercise of it. They will, like the foolish virgins, go forth with the wise to meet the bridegroom, keeping their lamps till their very death. The same principle of hypocrisy that made them dissemble in their life will make them speak many good words for a name at their death. Therefore beware of it; do not hunt after a name of religion, but seek to be sincere, to be really that which you seem to be. And whenever a challenge comes for this, rather entertain it and make some good use of it than shake it off; for though you could pass away undiscovered by man, God will find you out and discover you. I always say take notice of it as a mighty temptation, when folk take more pains to fair, and paint their condition over with fair words and shows, than to be real before God. So be upon your guard against it.

4. A fourth temptation is to thoughts of self-righteousness, which even some holy men at their

death have been more troubled with than any other temptation. It prevails much with formal professors (such as the Pharisees were) who, as they lived in conceit of it, so readily it cleaves to them at death. Such will be ready to say, "I thank God I kept the church. I was never harsh with my neighbors. I dealt truly and justly with all men. I was on the right side. I read, prayed, and kept the Sabbath." These are good things in themselves, I grant, but do not lay any weight upon them, and do not cling to them either in life or at death as the main foundation of salvation and consolation. Therefore, guard against it as a temptation whenever Satan comes to speak a good word to you regarding any merit or deserving.

5. The fifth and last is a temptation to doubting, yea, to desperation, which is not so frequent, I grant, yet it prevails with some who have lived very securely in their life. And when death comes the devil says, "You have never sought God in earnest all your days; and now that the time is gone, the door is shut and He will not hear you." This may through grace be answered, and it would not be strengthened by refusing the offer of God's grace even then, especially if some of the senses begin to fail and are taken away.

QUESTION 3. What do you think will be your thoughts at death? And I shall draw forth this question also into four or five questions:

1. What will you then think of the world, of all its pleasures, gains, and honors? In health and prosperity men have big and high thoughts of this and that vanity, project, and design; but what will you think of all outward prosperity, of barns full of corn, of cellars full of wine, of houses full of wealth and riches, of high places, honors, credit, and reputation in the world, when death comes to summon you to leave them all? The mind will not feed upon them then; the glory and

splendor of them will then grow dim and dark; they will then lose their blossom and flower; the taste and sweet relish of them will then quite vanish. Has not the experience of many men who swam in pleasures and abounded in wealth and honor verified the truth of this? Have they not found all then to be but vanity and vexation of spirit, and have they not some times proclaimed them to be so? Yea, before death, when under some great pain or sickness, or some quick and sharp challenge of conscience, all a man's riches, pleasures, and honors cannot then ease his mind.

2. What will be your thoughts of the chief grounds you have to build your peace on then? You can presume now, and have no doubt of your salvation; but at death your grounds will be narrowly sifted, and instead of a solid assurance you will scarcely get a fleeting thought of it. Instead of faith you will readily have doubting, and instead of hope you will have fear. How many at death have been made to think, and even to say, that they have been but beguiling themselves? And will not many of you, if God does not prevent it, think and say so? When you begin to look on eternity and God's justice, you will find that many things you have leaned on will not then abide the trial, nor be able to bear the weight of your soul's salvation, nor to answer the challenges which they answered in health. Hence is it that many at death will cry for a minister and for prayer, who cared little for their company and for that duty all their life. And when the minister comes they will then tell him they can do nothing, and indeed they can do nothing, till grace freely gives both to will and to do. But this bids you to beware of putting all off till death.

3. When you draw near your latter end, and death comes to sit down on your eyelids, when the eyes and ears begin to fail and eternity stares you in the face (for I suppose these persons will still have the exercise of

their judgment), what will be your thoughts then? May we not imagine the thoughts of many will be like those of the poor heathen emperor Hadrian, who spoke to his dislodging soul thus: "O poor soul, where are you going?" And what would you give for one more Sabbath then, for one more sermon then? When relations and neighbors are weeping about you, and you are groaning under a burden of sin and the fear of wrath, and also of pain and sickness—fain you would stay, but you may not, for the soul must go and not one hour's delay will be granted—what do you think you would give then, and at that hour to be allowed to come back again and stay a while here? And yet that hour is not far off from many of you; from some it is not a year away, and from others it may be not a month, yea, possibly not a week away.

4. What do you think will be the condition of the soul when it goes out and dislodges from the body, when the sentence shall be passed, and when legions of devils shall haul and drag the soul away to hell, the place of torment, that was thinking to go to heaven? What do you think will be the thoughts of such a soul who, in that person's lifetime, would have disdained and stormed to hear a minister or any other speak of hell, when it shall be thus unexpectedly seized on and hurried there? Do you think that there are no souls in hell, or that few or none at all are in hazard of being there eternally? If you will deny neither, but grant both, do you not then think that all they are infinitely wrong themselves who securely waste their time and do not think seriously on their dying in the Lord, which is the scope of all?

This doctrine lays before you life and death, heaven and hell. If you live and die in Christ, you shall get life and be eternally blessed; but if you live and die in your sins, instead of life you shall without all doubt meet with death, and such a death as has the wine of the wrath of God without mixture in the cup of His indignation, and torment, even eternal torment, without any the least intermission or mitigation, whereby you will be made everlastingly most miserable.

5. Do you not think it is of unspeakably great concern to think seriously on your living and dying in the Lord before death comes? Let me put this one question to you: what will be the thoughts of many in hell who have gotten fair warning of this ere it comes? Many of you, if grace does not prevent it, will then remember better on this preaching than you will do a day or two from now. You may reject and beat back a word now, but you will not get it beat back then. Rather, it will take hold of you; it will gall and torment you. The prophets do not live forever, said the prophet Zechariah in chapter 1, but the Word of the Lord will live forever. It will take hold of them who despised it; it will take them by the throat, as it were, and make them gasp eternally. May the Lord graciously knock hard at your hearts by this so important a truth that it may have access to you, and keep you from slighting it. "Blessed are the dead which die in the Lord; they rest from their labors, and their works do follow them."

3

The Way to True Misery

"Blessed are the dead which die in the Lord."
Revelation 14:13

There are some things of such concern to us that, if we go suitably, seriously, and singly about them, we can hardly speak too much of them, and therefore these four things that are called man's last things—death, judgment, heaven, and hell—have been so frequently recommended to Christians as the most constant subjects of their meditation. Among them all, death ought to have the first place, in order at least, it being the door whereby we enter into judgment. And as men die, so they shall rise, and may expect a final decision and sentence from the Judge about their eternal state. The Spirit's casting this in to divert John and the reader a little from following the series of the history puts a recommendation on it, and says that it is no digression for His people to bestow some serious thoughts on it.

The last thing I spoke to was a doctrine from the words as they lie, that they and they only are blessed who die in the Lord. Now, before I further prosecute the main uses of the doctrine, I shall speak a word to what is manifestly employed here. As they are truly blessed who die in the Lord, so they are exceedingly miserable who die out of Him in their sins; for the affirming of the one implies and supposes the other. It might follow on the former doctrine as a use; however, it is clearly in the words and commends dying in Christ to you all, and serves to stir you up to be serious to make

37

that sure. Therefore I exhort, beseech, and encourage you to count it of the greatest concernment unto you. It is to you men and women that I speak, and not to walls, to timber or stones. Do not sleep, neither let your minds wander, for I am speaking the words of truth so that many of you may not find the truth too late.

In prosecuting this doctrine, I shall speak a little to clear both branches of it, and then come to the use. The first branch is that there are many who do not die in Christ. This is clearly implied in the words. It is looked on as a rare thing in the spreading of the gospel, after the reign of antichrist, to find people dying in the Lord. He is a rare and happy man who dies in Him. The second branch of it is that those who die out of Him, in their sins, die exceedingly miserably. I shall confirm the first, and then speak a little to the explication of the second.

For the first, that there are many who do not die in Christ, it appears from Matthew 7:22 and Luke 13:24. These three things will confirm it abundantly:

1. The plain words of Scripture. Christ speaks of heaven as having, for those coming to it, a narrow way and a strait gate, so that few enter in thereat. And He speaks of hell and destruction as having a wide gate and a broad way into which many enter. When He speaks of the day of judgment, He says that many shall come to Him in that day and say, "Lord, Lord, open to us," to whom He will say, "Depart from Me. I never knew you." He will then set the goats on His left hand and send them thence into everlasting fire prepared for the devil and his angels.

These Scriptures speak not only of such as are outside the Church, but also, if not mainly, of many visible professors, yea, even of such as preached in His name. And yet the text says of them that they do not die in Christ.

2. If you look to the ordinary connection that is between men's living and dying, you will find that the way
of most men declares plainly that they do not die in the
Lord. As I will show, men's being and living in Christ
must precede their dying in Him; before they can die in
Him they must be in Him. I do not say that all must be
and live so many years in Him before they can die in
Him, but that they must be sometime in Him before
they can die in Him, and that they must live and put
forth some acts and breathings of a spiritual life, of the
life of faith in Him, even if it were but a few words to
God's glory and for other's edification; a few sighs,
groans, and looks to Him. We may see this in the thief
on the cross, though his time was very short.

And if this being and living in Christ must precede
dying in Him, if you compare it with most of your lives,
ah, how sad a prognostication does it give of what is
likely to be your way of dying? How many are there of
you who still live in your old black nature and were
never born again? If I could classify the lives of most, I
would ask:

(1) How many are living like atheists, not calling
upon God at all, casting off fear and restraining prayer
before Him? And as these live, so they die, for the most
part, either securely or desperately.

(2) How many live in formality and never knew
what it was to mortify the flesh, or sincerely to aim at
the power of godliness? And yet, says the Holy Ghost in
Romans 8:13, "If ye live after the flesh ye shall die, but if
ye through the Spirit mortify the deeds of the body ye
shall live." If grace is not in the heart, and if it is not at
all in the conduct, you cannot warrantably expect to die
in Christ. "Except a man be born again he cannot enter
into the kingdom of heaven." This is a large and great
class of people, and takes in all who live and die as they
were born, and do not seek after another life than that

which they brought with them into the world.

(3) How many are there who have some outward appearance and paint, and yet have no reality of religion within? Hereby they mock God and dissemble with men. It is to such that Christ speaks in John 8:21, and tells them that they shall die in their sins. Against this sort of men He denounces many woes.

(4) Are there not many who live without faith in Christ? Without it they cannot possibly please God neither living nor dying, and shall be damned if they continue so. The Lord says in John 3:18, "He that believes not is condemned already." Now when all these classes are laid aside, there will be but few left; all which proves abundantly the truth of the thing, and that there is but too good ground to think that there are very many who do not die in Christ.

3. A third ground of confirmation of this sad truth may be drawn from the ordinary way that most die in, and pass out of time into eternity. Oh, how many die securely, stupidly, and (as I said before) senselessly, and are no more affected with the thoughts of the immortality of their souls than if they had none at all? How many die presumptuously confident? How many ground their faith of dying well on wrong grounds? How many die doubtingly, not knowing what shall become of them? And how many die desperately? So, alas, there are but few among us who close their eyes like dying persons in Christ; and though we will not be peremptory in passing judgment upon or censuring particular persons as to their final state, yet all this shows that it is no common nor ordinary thing to die in the Lord.

As to the second branch of the doctrine, that those who die outside of Christ in their sins die in exceedingly great misery, it is also very clear; for as the happiness of them who die in Christ is inexpressibly great, so the misery and unhappiness of them who do not die in Him is also inexpressible. They are excluded and shut out from God and from all good, and have His wrath, His furious indignation, and His most severe justice pursuing them forever and ever.

We shall only consider it briefly in these two general headings: First, they are put out and secluded from the greatest happiness that can be imagined, and that in all the degrees of it. Second, they are concluded and put under the greatest misery that can be conceived, and that in all the degrees of it.

They are shut out from the greatest happiness, that is, from the fellowship of God who is the chief good, from conversing with the Lamb, glorious angels, and saints. They shall not have one saint in all their company; there is not, nor shall be, the least evidence of the love of God among all the thousands in hell, not one drop of cold water to cool the tongue of any of them who are tormented in these flames. They have judgment without the least mixture of mercy (James 1:13), and that forever without intermission. They shall never have the least glimmering of light nor the least mitigation of their pain. They shall have no rest night or day, and, which aggregates all to the very height and extremity, they have no gate out or hope of it, but lie in utter desperation under that felt eternal torment. It would be some lightening to the damned in hell if their torment were to continue but for some thousands of years, yea, or but for some millions of thousands of years. Poor Spira said that it would have been a comfort to him if hell had been put for twenty thousand years— but it is forever.

And if we look to the other part of it, they are in this hopeless condition under the greatest misery, drinking forever of the wine of the wrath of God without mixture in the cup of His indignation, which shall be both their meat and their drink. Their company shall be the devil and his angels. Oh, that we were serious in speaking and hearing and thinking on these things. The difference is both great and strange. Instead of sharing in the glory of God, of Christ, and of His angels, they will be sharing the torment of the devil and his angels. If it is a very evil, nay, the very worst condition, for a person to have enmity at God in the height, and to have God as an everlastingly irreconcilable enemy, furiously pursuing His quarrel—though without all passion in Him, yet with wonderful horror in the person that is thus plagued—it cannot surely be told to the full how inconceivably evil and miserable their condition is who die outside of Christ, nor what the hazard is that many of you are in in reference to it.

Application

USE OF EXHORTATION. Do not think that it is of light or little concern how you die, nor a thing that is unworthy of your most serious and painful endeavors to be made sure on good grounds that you shall die in Him. If it is of great concern to get heaven and escape hell; to be in God's company and not in the devil's forever; to have love and not hatred to God forever, and to have God's love to you and not His hatred forever (for death casts the balance)—then set yourselves seriously to obtain the one and eschew the other. And there is no way to win at it but by being, living, and dying in Christ.

USE OF REPROOF. This serves wonderfully to check and reprove the senseless, secure multitude that has the common profession of the faith of these things, and yet is utterly careless to have this most concerning question clearly, distinctly, convincingly, and satisfyingly answered, whether they shall die in the Lord. Certainly there are many of you, when your souls shall dislodge, who will find yourselves exceedingly mistaken in this matter. Oh, if we could pity and lament over the lamentable condition of many of you who are so senseless, stupid, and unconcerned, that whatever is spoken of the life to come and of the necessity of making your peace with God through Jesus Christ, it is as if it were spoken to so many stocks or stones, as to any suitable effect it has upon you, for who of many of you quit their profaneness, formality, hypocrisy, and security? Who through grace mends anything faulty and amiss, or sets more timeously and seriously about learning this great lesson of dying in the Lord? The supine, lazy, and gross neglect of all which bids you look for and lay your account to meet with the deeper, sorer, and sadder challenges at your death and appearance before God's terrible tribunal.

QUESTION. What is the reason that so many die out of Christ? How can this be, seeing they have no happiness, but so much and so great mystery by it? How does it come to pass that so many take the way of living and dying out of Him, and so few choose the way of living for Him and dying in Him?

ANSWER. To insist long and at large in answering this question would lead me to give reasons why men shun and decline the study of holiness and will be profane, why they despise the gospel and embrace the world and their lusts. But to leave such general things I shall speak a word or two more particularly and closely to this, why it is that so few die in the Lord.

REASON 1. The faith of these general truths—that there is a heaven and a hell, a life eternal and a judgment to come—is scarcely received by the multitude of the hearers of the gospel; yea, the very faith of their own dying in particular (though they know they will die, and though experience may teach them the same daily) does not sink into their hearts. Where are they who believe practically and with particular application that they will die and come to judgment, and that they shall be put into an eternal, unchangeable condition after death? And if this is not indeed believed, then, to allude to the apostle's words in 1 Corinthians 15, our preaching is in vain and your faith is but vain. That these things are not really believed I hinted at before when I began to speak on these words, and the practice of most undeniably proves it. For though all profess that they believe they will die, yet where are they who on this matter live beyond this day, and the next day, and the day following, and so on? So in effect they would live eternally here; and this is the root evil, or an evil root, that destroys many souls. Most people are like those spoken of in the days of Noah in Matthew 24, eating and drinking, marrying and giving in marriage, suffering one day to come and another to go till death comes and surprises them ere they are aware. And then they are confounded with the very first thoughts and appearances of death.

If men were seriously thinking on death, judgment, and a particular reckoning with God, and were really believing these things, is it possible they would thus delight themselves in their sinful lusts and pleasures, and have their affections so glued to a present world? No, certainly. The thoughts of death and judgment would put gall and wormwood in these things and embitter them.

REASON 2. A second reason may be drawn from people's gross mistakes about the right way of dying. They take dying in the Lord to be quite another thing than indeed it is; for even as folk mistake all other duties, so they mistake this. They take that for repentance, for faith, and for holiness, which is not repentance, or faith, or holiness indeed. They take that to be dying in the Lord which is not dying in Him.

And here I shall touch on four things which I think many take for dying in the Lord wherein yet they are exceedingly mistaken.

• They think that if they can die without any public scandal or known sin, or without challenges, and if they can get their presumptuous conceit and good opinion of themselves kept up to their grave (as if it were enough to say, "Lord, Lord, open to us"); and if they can go away calmly and quietly like these spoken of in Psalm 73:4, who have no bands in their death; that then they are well enough and die well. But this is a great mistake.

• They think that they die well if they die with a hope that it shall be well with them, and for this they will rigorously debate. And when Christ comes and tells them that they are beguiled, they will hardly trust Him, but rather, as it were, allege that He is mistaken and they are not the men. "What? Have we not eaten and drunken in Thy presence? Have we not heard Thee preach in our streets? Have we not been at many preachings and communions? We have always had a good hope towards God, and why should we now fear death?" Oh, the strong presumption that some die with! This is a great mistake.

• Some think that if they can die after some prayers and convictions, and that which they think to be repentance, all will be well. These things indeed, if they were real, would be good. But how many egregiously play the hypocrite in them? There are not a few who fancy that they have the grace of repentance because they have some sadness for sin, or a little anxiety, who yet never took seriously the corruption of their nature, and the quarrel that God has with them on that account, nor ever fled to Christ for refuge. Rather, they go away in their fit of carnal sorrow, and this is another great mistake.

• Some lay down a mold of religion of their own, and if they have a civil life with men, and some formality of religion towards God, they think themselves well enough. How many such are there who thus break their neck at death? Oh, sad mistake.

REASON 3. There are many who have some right thoughts and apprehensions of dying well, but they never seriously endeavor to bring them to practice. They do not seek to have their practice answerable to their light. In effect, they make a prisoner of their light by putting a guard of corrupt affections about it; for either they take an absolute dispensation to themselves, as to some particular lust or sin, or a liberty for such a time; and when that time is by they intend to quit and abandon such a lust and to think on death. But they will not quit it yet, nor prepare themselves for dying. They must first have their families in such a posture; they must have their children provided for and disposed of; they must have such or such a business put by their hand first—not knowing or considering that this hardens them, that they daily become further slaves to such things, and that judgment may surprise them unaware before their time comes. There are many who will not deny that a strict way of holiness is requisite, but they do not, they cannot prevail with themselves to fall about it yet. They are like that ill and slothful servant who, because the lord delayed his coming, went to eat and drink and to take his pastime. But his master came in an hour when he was not looked for, nor was the servant aware, and suddenly appointed him his portion with hypocrites. Ah, is it not thus with most, who, if they get a sickness or a cross dispensation, they think that Christ will bid a while longer, and so still they put off till it becomes too late.

REASON 4. Few are serious in going about these things that concern death, or in minding what will be their own case at death. Very few make conscience to examine themselves and search their bygone ways; and therefore they do not know their hazard. Among the many advantages of self-examination, this is a special one: it notably makes us fit, through God's blessing, for dying in the Lord; whereas, when it is neglected, souls are kept still securely sleeping and accounts lie over uncleared and unadjusted. They neither distinctly know their danger, nor their need of the remedy. All their prayers are by guess and haphazard, as it were; neither can they comfort themselves in any duty they go about. I name these things not only that you may know them, but that you may shun them, and that withal you may learn to draw some directions and duties out of them for your practice.

USE OF INSTRUCTION. Seeing that it is of such concern to die in the Lord, as it has eternal happiness depending upon it, let all of you seriously set yourselves to such a way of living that, when death comes, you may die in Him. If ever you would attain to this happiness, and eschew the misery of which you have been hearing, live in such a way that death may find you in Him.

To clear and press this a little, I shall speak a word to these three things: what dying in the Lord is; some rules or directions that all who would solidly comfort themselves in the hope of dying in the Lord may make use of and walk by in their life; and the necessity of taking these directions and walking according to them, even as you would have the comfort of these who die in the Lord, and of doing this speedily without delay or dallying.

There are three things or properties that go along with dying in the Lord, or with them who die in Him, that are exceedingly desirable. The first is dying willingly and cheerfully, not going to death as to a prison, but as through a trance to a palace. It is dying as old Simeon did in Luke 2: "Now, lettest Thou Thy servant depart in peace, for mine eyes have seen Thy salvation." Though death is the king of terrors, he hastens to it. Or it is dying as Paul did, who desired to be dissolved and to be with Christ as being best of all.

It is a dying with holy confidence and boldness, not with fear and terror or anxiety, doubtfully disputing what will become of us, but being confidently assured of a mansion in heaven. "We know," said the apostle in 2 Corinthians 5:1-2, "if the earthly house of this tabernacle be dissolved, we have a building of God, an house not made with hands, eternal in the heavens; for in this we groan earnestly, desiring to be clothed upon with our house which is from above." He was confident that at death his happy condition was but a beginning. To die in Christ makes a man set himself boldly against death and all its terrors.

It is dying not only with peace and quietness, but with complacency and satisfaction. So even if the soul had its wish it desires no more, a man does not fret or complain that he is taken from a good and plentiful estate, from a fine and commodious dwelling, from friends and relations, from honor and reputation in the world; but he dies with contentment, being fully satisfied with his right to look to the fair inheritance above. This we may see in David, who sweetly says and sings in 2 Samuel 23:5, "This is all my salvation and all my desire, although He makes not my house to grow." And therefore he will (Psalm 23) walk resolutely through the valley of the shadow of death and fear no evil, because the Lord is with him.

Indeed, it is no small matter to die willingly, cheerfully, confidently, and boldly, and with quietness, contentment, and satisfaction. But the grounds that these three flow from mainly answer and determine the question, for it is not a counterfeit willingness, nor a natural boldness or manliness of spirit, nor a carnally secure peace and quietness flowing from being senseless, but such willingness, boldness, and quietness as come and flow from three pregnant grounds:

• From peace with God through Jesus Christ, the soul having really fled for refuge to Jesus Christ and committed itself to Him. Faith says that is a good, sure, thorough, and everlasting bargain, and so the man rests on it and has peace.

• From a good conscience giving a good testimony, which is an excellent ground to come before God's judgment with. A man needs the testimony of a good conscience either in respect of an endeavored blameless life, or, if the man does not have so good a conscience in that respect, but many failings and so many challenges, yet he has a good conscience in respect to its being sprinkled with the blood of Jesus, through whom all his failings and transgressions are pardoned, which also takes in a good conscience of sincere endeavor to study holiness.

• From a lively and distinct frame of spirit, whereby faith has some present acting on Christ, and on the everlasting covenant even in death, that the soul is by and by to meet with. There is a difference among these three. The first of them is simply and absolutely necessary; and the second is necessary also in one of the two aforementioned respects; the third may not be always necessary (for a believer may die in the rage of a fever, in a fit of high distemper, or in a stupefying palsy). Yet it is always to be pursued and sought after, with submission to God's blessed will; and it conduces much to the believer's confidence and comfort to have some present actings of faith in a distinct way on Christ and on the covenant of grace.

I suppose now that this is such a sweet condition to die in as there is none of you but would desire to be in it at your death. But let me say this, most do not take the right way to attain it.

Therefore, in the second place, let me speak a little to those rules and directions that you must seriously, and in the strength of grace, endeavor to live by, without which you cannot, with well grounded confidence, promise to yourselves these comforts at death, and the blessedness that follows it.

I shall first speak of that which is not the way of dying in the Lord. Then I shall propose to you the way wherein you should walk in order to attain this desirable end.

It is not dying in the Lord to die in external quietness, and with all our friends about us, or in a sort of calmness with little pain or sickness. Many heathens, many carnal and civil men, and many hypocrites, have died that way. It is but a common outward thing, and many may and do slip quietly into the pit.

Nor is it being taken up with bare wishings and desirings to die so, nay, nor with some esteem of dying in the Lord. It is good indeed to wish it, desire it, and esteem it; but Balaam, who had a most miserable exit and made a very wretched end, came that far (Numbers 24), and yet this is a great part of many folks' religion, yea, almost all of it, who will now and then commend it when in a good mood.

Nor is it dying in the Lord to have some cold-rise prayers to die so, and to be "good friends with God," as we used to speak. There are none so graceless but, seeing that they must leave the world, would rather be in heaven than in hell, and will readily have some general desires after it, and words of prayer for it. But that will not do the turn, for many will seek to enter who shall not be able (Luke 13:24). Many will pray to be taken to heaven who never walked, nor loved to walk, in the right way to it.

Nor is it dying in the Lord to take some pains in the externals of holiness, to be hearing preachings and frequenting communions. If that is all, it will not do the turn either. It will not be sufficient that you heard Christ preach and sat at one table with Him; half of holiness is no holiness. To be an almost Christian will not you make a Christian indeed. There is a necessity of being a Christian altogether; to have half holiness and be almost a Christian only will be but to be half saved, and that will be indeed no salvation, but will end in eternal damnation. So that cannot be dying in the Lord.

Nor is it to die with a persuasion in our own mind, though it is ill-grounded, that we are in Him and that all shall be well. Many take themselves to be well and in a good and safe condition because they believe it and fancy that they are so; and they are very unwilling and loathe to let themselves think ill of themselves. When we speak then of dying in the Lord, it must be such as will abide God's trial, and it is not he who commends himself, but he whom God commends who will abide his trial and be approved.

QUESTION. You may ask, so what then will do it?

ANSWER. I shall as I promised commend to you some rules to walk by for attaining this end of dying in the Lord:

1. Make your peace with God through faith in Christ, and see that you are not living with a standing quarrel between God and you. For it is by faith that we are united to Him, and without faith we cannot be in Him, and so cannot possibly die in Him.

2. Do not only have faith in Christ, and your peace made with God through Him, but know that you have it, to know in whom you have believed. This is not as

essential as the former, yet it is hardly possible to die comfortably and confidently without it. Therefore Christians are exhorted in 2 Peter 1:10: "Give diligence to make your calling and election sure."

3. Be exercised to keep a good conscience in all things, and always towards God and towards men. It is impossible in an ordinary way to die well unless folks endeavor seriously and singly to keep a good conscience all their life, to square the same according to the rule of the Word, and to walk suitably to their profession. All these three are put together by the Apostle Peter in 2 Peter 1:5. He wants them to whom he writes to add to their faith the exercises of the other graces of the Spirit. Then in verse 10, he exhorts them to give diligence to make their calling and election sure; and by so doing, he assures them that an entrance shall be ministered to them into the everlasting kingdom, which is as if he had said, "By fastening your faith on Christ, by the exercise of grace, by studying to make your calling and election sure, and by well doing, a wide door shall be made to you at death to enter into heaven, and ye shall have the greatest comfort and confidence to lay down your life." On the contrary, when Christians neglect the fastening and fixing of their faith, the exercise of grace, and the making of their calling and election sure, the entry is strait and difficult. And others who altogether neglect these things find the door quite shut and no entry at all.

If there were no more spoken but these three words, to be in Christ by faith, to live in Him by the exercise of faith and other graces, keeping a good conscience towards God and men, and to make your calling and election sure, they might furnish you with work and duty to take you up all your days. And they may also serve to convince and reprove many who vainly entertain themselves with the hope and expectation of dying in Christ,

but who do not at all take to this way of being and living in Him. We must go with a blackened face and a
stopped mouth to the throne of grace, and cordially
close with Christ's offer, being content to adhere to
Him for righteousness, and utterly to renounce our
own. Then, in a way of diligence in duty, and by the
fruits of a new nature and life, we are to evidence our
union with Him.

This is the very marrow and substance of what we
would be at, and that which is the hinge of our salvation, even the right exercise of faith for righteousness,
the right exercise of grace for sanctification, and the
right setting of ourselves ere death comes, to have the
grounds of our interest be sure and clear. But such of
you as have taken no pains to walk in this way, but still
walk on and continue in your own old carnal way, cannot warrantably expect the benefits and comforts that
flow from faith in Christ and from walking in Him, and
these are to die in Him and to reign with Him. Now
may God Himself bless these words and make them
useful to you.

4

Directions for Dying in the Lord

"Blessed are the dead which die in the Lord."
Revelation 14:13

It is an easy matter to speak and hear of the most spiritual and highly important truths in comparison to what it is to make them practical; and hence it comes to pass that so many speak and hear of them, and that so few practice them. The nearer the truths or duties press upon us for the mortification of our lusts, to abstract us from the world, or to prepare us for dying, the more loath and reluctant we are to engage in the practice of them and to keep close at it. It is a hard and difficult business to be both living and dying at once—though every man living may be said to be dying daily in so far as he is hastening to it. And therefore, seeing what follows concerns your practice, and is the main and most material use of this great doctrine, harken diligently and give ear to what I am to say from God on this important subject, with a serious purpose and resolution to practice; for it will not otherwise be of advantage to you. So prepare yourselves though grace to hear that you may firmly resolve to keep that which is of so great and everlasting concern to you.

I last commended to you the right way of living so that, when death comes, you may have some well-grounded hopes of dying in the Lord. I spoke of what dying in Him is, and showed what it was to have solid faith and clearness of interest in Christ, cheerfulness and comfort, quietness and satisfaction in dying, a most desirable and comfortable condition when we enter the lifts with death, even to have this confidence that we are in Him and shall die in Him.

I then gave some directions that are so many steps to attain this comfortable end of dying in the Lord. Now I wish to prosecute them a little further, through the help of God's grace. Before I could be particular in directions, I showed that these things: (1) Flee to Christ by faith, make peace with God through Christ by faith, and make peace with God through Him. (2) We must endeavor to make our calling and election sure by well doing, for though our justification before God does not depend in this, yet much of our comfort and confidence depends on it, and it is no doubt our duty to labor to make it sure. (3) There must be a holy walk whereby we may have a good conscience at Christ's appearing; for there can never be boldness and confidence where there is a stinging conscience within, and challenges for sinning against light.

If I were to speak more particularly on how to live so that you may die well, if I could say all that might be said to this purpose, it would lead me to speak of all the duties of holiness, and that with respect to all the conditions of our life, sickness and health, prosperity and adversity; to our particular and general callings; and to all events. For as we carry in these, so we may expect to die. But these being general, I shall pass them by and only propose some directions regarding men's dying in Christ as the great scope of this doctrine.

DIRECTION 1. Seek to establish yourselves in the faith of these general truths that concern your dying; especially seek to be established and confirmed in the faith of death, judgment, and eternity, wherein it will be either well or ill with you forevermore. This is not only to have a general conviction of the truth of these, but by meditation to draw them down to particular application to yourselves: that you will die; that after death you will come to judgment and be eternally happy or miserable. For as I said before, one of the great evils that nourishes atheism is men's living as if they were never to die. So it is a foundation of well doing to solidly believe the truth about death, judgment, and eternity; and they can never live well who do not lay for a ground that they will die and come to judgment, and who do not consider what will readily be their challenges at death. They should seek to answer them now, and see what may be their temptations so that they may guard against them. If you did these things, you would be established in the faith of these generals truths, and would endeavor to draw death and judgment near to you. You would pursue them close in your meditation.

Suppose that death were approaching you this very night. Consider with yourselves, if you dare, appearing before God's tribunal to be judged. More of this in our thoughts would help us, through God's blessing, to mortify lusts, and to give death little to do when it comes. But, the truth is, most never think seriously on death, and because they do not desire another life than the present, they shun to think of death. I commend the necessity of this to you from the great averseness that your carnal hearts and humors have from the serious and flayed thoughts of it. I pose this question to you who are given to pleasure: Can you endure to think of dying? And you who are gluttons and indulge yourselves with the world, do you think on that word from Christ, "Thou fool, this night thy soul shall be taken from thee, and whose shall these things be?" You who are profane, do you think on that sad sound of the trumpet, "Arise, dead, and come into judgment"? That word from Job is fitting to be carried along with you: "I know Thou wilt bring me unto death," though the good man was mistaken in thinking he would die at that time; yet he knew that he would die ere long and be brought unto judgment after death. Thus he carried along with him the thoughts of it. And if we would be induced to prepare for death by these thoughts, how few of us would be found to mind it, though it is of everlasting concern? Ah, how few hours are taken up with thinking about it? If you were to come before men or a human court with a cause that much concerned you in the world, how would you think of it beforehand, and then think of it again? Yet the most momentous of these matters are but trifles compared with this great question of how you shall die and appear before the great God at His judgment seat.

DIRECTION 2. Though all duties of holiness are required, yet there are some particular duties that you would in a special manner make conscience of (without neglecting any other called-for duty) as having a special influence on preparation for dying, and as coming nearest (to say so) to death, though much slighted. There is, first, the duty of self-searching and examination. If men (as Solomon exhorts) should see to the state of their herds and their flocks, much more should they see to the condition of their souls? Is it possible, do you think, to die confidently and comfortably if you are not acquainted with the state of your spiritual affairs, and do not endeavor to have your accounts with God stated and adjusted? If there is a plague on men, it is the neglect of this; and if there is a restraint on their spirits from unsuitable latitudes and looseness, it is the conscionable practice of this duty. That which makes death so terrible to many is their living some thirty, some forty, some fifty, some sixty years without having ever endeavored to make their accounts right with God.

Second, there is the exercise of repentance (which

is, alas, a rare thing even among Christians in these days). This is a special duty to be gone about in order to our dying in Christ, so that when we see ourselves wrong in anything (as many wrongs may be easily found in the aforementioned search), we do not let them lie over, but are earnest with God till we get a discharge—and that cannot be had till repentance is exercised. Where this grace of repentance is, faith is always with it. It makes the heart tender, and removes challenges which make death terrible. Repentance is also a great enemy to security, presumption, and pride, and keeps the heart withal melting, and much in pouring out itself before God. The lack of it in these days is responsible for the coldness of our duties in worship, and for the carnality of our walk. However, they who would die in the Lord should study to be found much in the exercise of this grace (we do here indifferently design these as "duties" or "graces"); for if repentance is called for when the kingdom of heaven is near, then surely it is called for when death is near. And there is nothing more required than a kindly, penitent heart as a spur to fly to Jesus Christ when we meet Him at death.

Third, the exercise of mortification is a painful but profitable duty. It is to be crucified to the world, to die to our lusts and carnal delights. By mortification I mean not only that which takes away the dominion of sin and sets us to the study of holiness, but that which plucks up the roots of sin also slays the motions of it and weeds it out of the heart. It is that which puts you to mortify your distempers and passions of envy, anger, pride, inordinate desires, and so forth, and to seek to have your affections heavenly, which notably fits for dying in the Lord.

A fourth duty that should be carefully practiced is sobriety. "Let your moderation," said the apostle, "be known to all men; the Lord is at hand." While mortifi-

cation looks much to things that are in themselves sinful and unlawful (I say "much," though I will not say
"only"), sobriety looks to things lawful in themselves.
Insobriety is the bane and plague of many who, being
so glued to the things of this world, to those delights
and pleasures which are lawful in themselves, and
whereof a moderate use is allowed, are entangled and
fettered with them, and made as unfit for dying by their
insobriety in them as by their doing of some things
that are in themselves sinful, Oh, how inordinate love
to children, friends, lands, houses, farms, oxen, and to
the married wife unfit them for dying! Therefore the
apostle exhorts Christians in 1 Peter 1:13 to "gird up the
loins of your mind," to be sober and hope to the end;
for when men are unsober in the use of the creatures,
they are like those who have long garments which im-
pede them in their walking and at their work. When
the affections hang loose and drag on the earth, and
the things that are in it, and the mind takes liberty to
wander and rove after these things, the man cannot be
busy at his main work or make progress in his journey
to heaven. But sobriety fits him for his works and
makes the way easy to him; it makes him well content
with his house or place and station, and with whatever
his condition and lot are in the world. It does not allow
his affections to be entangled with them; it makes him
so to use this world as not abusing it.

The apostle exhorts us in 1 Corinthians 7 to have a
sort of sanctified denyedness to a lawful use of the creature comforts, so that the heart is not glutted and sati-
ated with them. From this our blessed Lord Jesus most
powerfully dissuades in Luke 21:34, where He says,
"Take heed lest at any time your hearts be overcharged
with surfeiting and drunkenness, and the cares of this
life, and so that day come upon you unawares." There
He plainly insinuates (which is strange and little be-

lieved and considered) that there is an overcharge by cares about the things of this life that are lawful in themselves, as well indisposing and unfitting for death and judgment, as an overcharge with the surfeiting and drunkenness is. This sobriety prepares for dying in the Lord, to which preparation on the contrary an overcharge with worldly cares is a mighty impediment, as these words of our Lord put beyond all debate. This is especially true when these two are trusted together, a distempered mind with such worldly cares within, and many temptations and stumbling blocks from without.

DIRECTION 3. They who would die in the Lord should carry the thoughts of death along with them, as if every day and moment were their last, as if they were just now to appear before God, and as if they were holily indifferent what hour or moment He would call upon them. For God has set (as to our knowledge of it) no time precisely to our living here; it is observed by some on Ecclesiastes 3 that there is a time for every thing, a time to be born, a time to die, a time to laugh, and a time to weep, but there is none for living. For none can say I must or I shall live till tomorrow; and therefore he bids the porter watch, and would have all standing with their armor on them in a watchful posture, waiting for their Lord's coming so that He does not come on them unaware. "Do that now which you would be found doing when death comes" has been an old and excellent saying.

QUESTION. Is it possible that a believer can always actually remember Christ's coming and carry the thoughts of death along with him?

ANSWER. It is in this duty as in others, as when it is said do all to the glory of God, it is not so to be understood as if we could actually mind it all along in everything we do. Our minds are but finite, and so are unable actually to mind many things or different things in the same instant of time or at once. That is impossible, but as there is a habitual minding of the glory of God, so there is a habitual minding of Christ's appearance, which implies these three things:

• That when we resolve to wait for and carry ourselves suitable to the expectation of His appearing, and to do nothing that we would shun or think shamefully of, or would not desire to be found doing if He were appearing, is in effect to be continually on our watch.

• That when ever we find ourselves napping, we stir ourselves up to an actual minding of it, and endeavor to square the actions of our life accordingly, asking our own hearts if we dare do this or that if He were to appear, and accordingly to be swayed with the awe of His appearing.

• That in our ordinary walk, we are often reviving the thoughts of Christ's appearing, putting ourselves often in mind of this rule, even to walk so as if He were immediately to appear. Hence believers are often called in Scripture "waiters for and lovers of His appearing." Hence also the duty of watching is so frequently commended to them. So, then, we would not have this so universally to be understood as if believers were to do nothing more, nor if it were spoken by a voice from heaven that they would presently die, or that Christ were presently to appear; for then they would leave many actions undone, and leave off lawful journeys and voyages, and other actions they are called to. But the meaning is that we endeavor to be found in or at nothing we will think shamefully of when He appears, and in all things always to keep a good conscience, a conscience void of offense towards God and man.

DIRECTION 4. Those who would die in the Lord should be quickly acquainting themselves with the cross of Christ and not seeking after a pampered life, or to have the world at their will, but learning to fold, bow,

and stoop to difficulties and straits. Not that I would
have any procuring crosses for themselves, but as they
should not procure them, so they should not peremptorily determine to eschew them when the Lord calls to
take them on and bear them. But they should carry
along a resolution to accept crosses when they come.
When they come, they should neither with sinful anxiety seek to shun them, nor should they lie down dis-
couraged under them, but deny themselves, take up
their cross pleasantly and cheerfully, and follow Christ.
They who have personal freedom from crosses should
kindly sympathize with them who are under the cross.
Hence Solomon says that it is better to be in the house
of mourning than in the house of feasting (Ecclesiastes 7:2). There is a greater good to be had there than
in the house where there is banqueting, reveling, and
carousing. The reason is because few living in
prosperity are content and disposed to die, and adversity best looses folks' grips on the world. Oh, it is
hard to be glutting in the things of the world, to live in
a prosperous and plentiful condition, and not be with-
drawn thereby from spiritual things. Therefore the
cross and dying to the world is so much commended;
for little crosses are, as it were, bits of death or little
deaths and pieces of the curse as well as death itself
(though by the death of Christ they are turned into
blessings to believers). And if we are habitual to these
little deaths, there will be a much easier yielding to the
great death, and less to do when it comes.

DIRECTION 5. Study to die daily, and that is drawn
from the apostle's words in 1 Corinthians 15:31: "I
protest by your rejoicing, which I have in Christ Jesus
our Lord. I die daily." This not only sets out his hazard
daily, but his seeking to prevent death; in dying while
he was living and ere death came. And that implies:

• A conviction carried along with him of the necessity of dying.

• A looking on the continual hazard of dying.

• A preparation for and continual readiness to die.

• An activeness in preparing to die, or an acting of death before death comes. We should follow the same way, and be frequently putting ourselves before God's bar, considering how we will answer death's call, bowing our stubborn humor so that it may not be found untractable at death, doing that every day that we would be found doing when death comes, studying to have all things in that order that we would desire to have them in then, and habituating ourselves (as I said) to dying. When we go to our prayers in the morning, we should put ourselves in such a posture as if we were no more to go abroad in the world; and lying down at night, as if we were not to rise again in the morning; and when we speak or do, to speak and do like men who do not have a long time to live after our speaking or doing.

DIRECTION 6. Put into practice what your own conscience, your light according to the Scriptures, and the means you have, holds out as necessary for making and keeping your peace with God, and avoiding a quarrel between Him and you. This ordinarily is one of the main challenges that meets folks at death, that they have suspended the practice of many things they were convinced of, that they have shifted, delayed, and put off seasons and opportunities of called-for duties, and have sat down on this side of them; that they have not reformed such faults as they were convinced of. It is commonly said of laws that we need one law to make other good laws be put into execution, and so we need one direction to help us to make other directions practical. Ecclesiastes 9:10: "Whatsoever thy hand findeth to do, do it with all thy might, for there is no work, nor knowledge, nor wisdom, nor device in the grave whither thou goest." We are all hasting on towards our grave, and there is no doing duties or mending faults there. Therefore, whatever the light of the Word, and of our conscience well informed thereby, clears to be duty, we should be serious and diligent in doing it, and in doing it without delay. If this one thing were made conscience of, it would do more, through God's blessing, than many. Your consciences are convinced, I suppose, that the former directions are very helpful, and that such as live thus will die the better. But, alas, many of you do not so much as think on them, let alone practice them! They may not be in your thoughts till eight days from now, if then, and when it is so, to what purpose are all directions, for what use do they serve? Are they not useless unless they are put in practice? Therefore, do not make this a thing of little concern. Death is the door to heaven, and death is at the door. Living well is the way to dying well. And as you would live and die in the Lord, you should lay weight on these directions, and fall about the practice of them in the strength of His own grace.

But before I proceed any further, though there may be a conviction that what has been said is all true, yet there will be an inward murmuring against it with many profane persons. And such will readily make two objections:

OBJECTION. "If none die well but such as take themselves to such a way of living, who will or can die well? Such a life is impossible to us; therefore we will hold on in our own way and hope well." Many, when they hear such doctrine, are ready to think and say as they did in John 6:60: "This is a hard saying, who can hear it?" They will say, "We shall by this means be restrained in our liberty; we shall thus be always frequenting the house of mourning, and never allowed once to laugh or smile" (although my meaning is not to keep men from being merry and cheerful when called to be so, but to them keep from being carnal, and to set just bounds to them in their mirth).

ANSWER. Is this the truth of God, that such as would die in Him must aim and endeavor to live as we have said? Is living well the way to dying well, and dying well the gate to glory? If so, will it then be a satisfying answer to God to tell Him that, though this way of living is the way chalked out by Thee for dying well, yet we cannot close with it; we cannot walk in it; it is so uneasy and so narrow a way? If it is God's way, will you put it off so? Or will you carve out another way than God has carved out to you?

Let me ask such, is not the gate strait and the way narrow that leads to heaven and eternal life? Will you not therefore go to heaven through such a gate and way? And is not the way of living so as to die well and in the Lord the way to heaven, and must it not have difficulty in it?

Let me say to such that this way is but difficult and uneasy to corrupt nature, to a proud and carnally delicate heart that cannot endure in the least to be disquieted in the enjoyment of its sensual pleasures and delights, and to a sinful selfish humor that will not stoop to God. Yet to such as love to walk in this way, all the duties are possible and the difficulties sufferable through grace; yea, it is throughout a most pleasant path and way (see Philippians 4:13 and Proverbs 3:17).

OBJECTION. "All the things you speak of may be true, nay, we cannot deny but that they are true, yet we may not be doing all this and yet hope through God's mercy to win heaven. Have not many who have lived even as we do died well and been saved?" Such will readily have the thief on the cross to cast up, which would in reason speak to them for their reclaiming; and from this they profanely conclude that they may go on their own way, and yet hope to mend and grow better at length and so to get mercy when they die.

ANSWER. O you graceless and profane wretch! Is that the use you make of mercy, to sin because God is merciful, and to sin that grace may abound? Is that the end of God's revealing His grace and mercy, to make Him a minister of sin? How can you look mercy in the face who so abuse mercy? And yet, oh, how common is it among profane souls to sin because God is merciful, to abuse His grace and make Him, as I said, a minister of sin! Consider it, if you will dare to look grace and mercy in the face, who have thus stumbled and broken your necks on them.

Though there are some to whom God has given mercy to at their death, yet how many are they who have sinned presumptuously and have gotten mercy? The thief on the cross, it is true, got mercy; but did he ever despise and abuse God's grace and mercy as you do? It is one thing to sin out of infirmity, and humbly to pray for and expect mercy; but it is quite another thing to sit through warnings, and profanely to turn the grace of God into wantonness, and yet to have a presumptuous hope of mercy.

How many are there in hell, and how few are there in heaven, who have lived as you do? God's judgment has come upon them and surprised them, so that they never got leave to repent or seek after God's mercy; and they are now smarting for delaying to embrace the offer of mercy, for their despising of it, and now they cannot mend it. How many are like the rich glutton crying in the place of torment, who, if they were permitted to speak to you, would say, 'Go tell our brethren so that they do not put off time, and so that they do not dally with the offers of grace and mercy as we did, lest they come into this place of torment with us."

Who ever got mercy to whom their sin has not been

bitter to them? And will you continue in that which has been so bitter to others? If ever you get mercy, you must come to it through the way of repentance; and it shall be more bitter to you than all the pleasure you had in sin was sweet to you.

The last thing I wish to do is to give some considerations to press the necessity of taking these directions, and of walking according to these rules, so that you may not be unfruitful hearers, but doers of this truth; for it is practice that is the life of religion, and if anything ought to be practiced, surely it is to learn the right art of dying in the Lord. And therefore, that you may not decline in it, consider first whether or not the authority of God and His Son Jesus Christ lays out this doctrine. If there is a command that all who expect to die in Christ should live in Him, and if to die in Him is a duty, then to make use of the means and directions that conduce to it, must likewise be a commanded duty, and these must be the true and faithful sayings of God. It is a wonder that you can have anything to say against them, for you cannot deny them to be the truths of God. And yet, as it is Psalm 50, many of you "cast them behind your backs." You will not bow a knee to God in prayer when you go home; you will not so much as ask yourselves what posture your soul is in for all that has been or can be said. Remember that you will have God and not us to make an account unto; and therefore any of you who have consciences, and the least measure of tenderness in them, mind these duties, or else know that you shall be the more inexcusable. If I dare confidently press any truth upon you, it is this one concerning dying in Christ, and holiness as the way to it. It is the sum and scope of all our preaching, which will only do you good if it works to this end. And therefore let us, with all earnestness, implore you to think more seriously on your dying in Christ and, in order to that, on your living in Him and to Him so that you may have boldness at His appearing. Otherwise, I seriously and solemnly protest unto you in the name of God that you shall never see His blessed face, nor enjoy His blessed fellowship.

The second consideration is taken from your own great advantage, and the mighty concern that is in giving obedience to these directions. Though there is a second death to them who do not make ready of the first, yet there is but one death to all of you as to the final sentence, and upon this depends heaven and hell and the eternal condition of your immortal souls, whether they shall be under the curse of God drinking of the cup of His wrath forever, or under His blessing drinking the cup of His love forever; whether they shall be in the status of enemies or in the status of friends; whether they shall enjoy God's company or have the company of devils. And do you think there is no difference between blessedness and misery? Are you not concerned which of these two shall befall you and be your lot forevermore? Are you beasts that have no immortal souls? Or are you heathens who never heard of the right way to heaven and happiness, that you should thus walk on in the broad way that leads to hell and destruction, and turn your backs upon the narrow way because it is narrow, and so willfully precipitate yourselves into the bottomless pit, and into the deep gulf of God's curse and wrath forever? However little you may think of these things now, yet you shall, if you do not look to it, find the certain and sad truth of them one day to your eternal cost.

A third consideration is drawn from the great work that there is regarding death. When it comes to die, the immortal soul must be dislodged and leave the body, and will not possibly be kept any longer in it. You never made such a voyage; you never had such a piece of work in hand as this will be found to be, when infirmities of the body grow on you quickly and at a great height; when the encumbrance and fashion of the things of the world; when the affection of relations and friends; when eternity stares you in the face; when the devil, that great accuser not only of the brethren, but of all other men, waits with his libels; when the Law passes the sentence and curses every transgressor; when Christ's dreadful sentence, "Depart from Me, ye cursed," are all to be met with and encountered at once; when the conscience within will be clamoring to you that you were not at all solicitous and careful to eschew that sad sentence—and besides all these you will yet have a greater party to deal with than your conscience, even the great God, the just and righteous Judge of all the earth (and it is a fearful thing to fall into the hands of the living God!); when withal you shall have a multitude of challenges and temptations to enter the lifts with, this will be found another sort of thing than a journey to London, or a voyage to Holland, France, or Spain, or to the East or West Indies. Do you who have spent all your life in vanity think that an hour or two, or a little time at death, will be enough to prepare you to encounter it? Oh, sad and soul-ruining mistake! Are there not many poor, wretched souls who, when death comes, are forced to wish, "Oh, if we had another lifetime to live, we would spend it better!" And with such a wish as that, poor souls, they slip away.

Fourth, consider the connection that God has established between your dying in the Lord and following these directions, between holiness and happiness. Now holiness is not speaking some good words when you come to die; otherwise why should it be pressed so much in your life? The end of holiness is heaven and happiness, and the end of the broad way of profanity and formality is hell and destruction. It is true, as I have often said, that God may pluck some by a miracle of His grace out of the broad way at their death, but they are very few with whom He so deals. The way to destruction is broad and easy, and many walk in it. Oh, how is this road beaten by multitudes of passengers, and usually as men live so they die. If they live wickedly, they die accursedly and fall into perdition. Hence is that proverb: "Such a life, such an end." A man who is worldly-minded, or presumptuous and self-conceited in this life, ordinarily dies so. And can you promise yourselves a comfortable death if you live profanely or hypocritically? Do not be deceived, God will not be mocked; for if you sow to the flesh all your life, you shall most certainly of the flesh reap corruption at your death. Know therefore and believe the absolute necessity of living well, of living in and to the Lord, if you would die well and in the Lord.

Fifth, consider and think seriously upon the great hazard you are in of spiritual judgments if you neglect holiness and the following these directions in your life. Be afraid of blinding, of hardening, of delusion, and of a reprobate mind. Be afraid that though you should get a long time before death, that yet you may never get grace to repent who thus delay and put it off so long. If you then would die well and prevent such plagues, live holily. But if you do not care if you die miserably or not, then go on in your profanity and presumption, notwithstanding the hazard of being thus plagued, and of perishing at last, all on the fancied hope of mercy. For in one of these ways you must live and die.

But again, consider what spiritual judgments you may fall under while you are delaying. You do not know but that commission may come forth from God to His Word and messengers to make your heart fat, your eyes blind, and your ears heavy. Such a sad commission the prophet Isaiah got in the sixth chapter of his prophecy to many of his then hearers. It may be a challenge has been resisted, or a motion of the Spirit quenched at this very time, and who knows but that you may never henceforth meet with another one that shall do you good? Are there not many judgments of this kind rained on sinners daily? Are not many preached into being blind, deaf, and hard, so that the plainest, clearest, and most home-pressed truths have no more influence on them than upon as many sticks or stones? And why is this, I pray? Is it not from not making use of the light held forth to you from the Word of God, and from resisting, stifling, and smothering the challenges and motions of the Spirit you have had? Because of this God smites you with senselessness.

Sixth, consider what possible advantage there is or can be in delaying so necessary a work, and what certain prejudice there is in it. There is no advantage at all, for the longer you continue to delay, the further behind you are, the further out of the way you are, and the greater the difficulty there will be to get yourselves recovered. There will be still more guilt contracted, more challenges to deal with, and greater labor needed to get your spirits put into a good frame which you have so much and so long distempered. Yea, it will be a piece of a begun hell to you when you consider how you have brought yourselves to such a woeful necessity of hassling, mangling, and spoiling all that work and business that you should have gone about so deliberately, orderly, quickly, and carefully in the time of your health. So that all your advantage will be but more sin, and that will bring on a greater heap of desperate sorrow and wrath.

You will not only have no advantage, but you will have much prejudice by it; for beside what has been said, you cannot comfortably answer death's call and summons to appear before the tribunal of the great

Judge. How many of you, if you were to die just now and never to go out of this church alive, would not have peace and comfort at your death? If the walls of this house were shaking, would not horror take hold on you as pangs of a woman in travail? It may be that some who are believers in Christ would be somewhat disquieted and a little surprised; yet they would soon through grace recollect themselves and be composed. But could most of you lay down your life with peace, calmness, and comfort, if death should thus come upon you now or before tomorrow? You are not sure what may befall you ere you go home, nor when you lie down if ever you shall rise again. And is it possible that you can have peace or comfort on solid grounds when death comes if you are not found having your peace made with God through Jesus Christ, and walking in the way of holiness? It will be but poor and cold comfort then to think that you have made such an advantageous bargain in the world, that you have such a land estate or so much money, such a commodious house, or such a well furnished shop, that this one word will mar all that comfort: "Fool, this night thy soul shall be required of thee, and whose then shall all these things be?"

Seventh, consider the particular crosses, infirmities, and afflictions you are under, and may be shortly under, which may put you in mind of dying, and invite you to make for a change to the better. Now you are in health, but within a little while you may fall sick. Now you are in safety, but by and by you may be in hazard. Do not so many changes call on you aloud to make for an unchangeable estate, and to endeavor to make sure that it is a happy one?

And now that I have spoken to both directions and considerations, pressing and enforcing the practice of them, to order our life and walk with a due regard to dying in the Lord, I am afraid that it shall be but as water spilled on the ground, and will but little further the conviction and edification of many of us, which God only can prevent. And therefore I shall close with a word to two sorts of you:

The first is to you who are struck deaf and dead with the spiritual judgments of God, who no more regard or mind your immortal souls than if you had none at all; who live rather like beasts than like reasonable men and women, or like pagans rather than like Christians. This comes through carnal joviality and mirth in some, through profanity and mocking of piety in others, through idleness in still others, through the earthly-mindedness and groveling in the world that is in some, and through the security, formality, and hypocrisy that reigns in the greatest part of men. I assure you in the name of the Lord that death is coming. And God will not be mocked; as you sow, so you shall reap.

Do you think it sufficient preparation for death, or a suitable readiness to die, to laugh and sport and play over your time, or to have your buildings going up and your bargains going on? Do not beguile yourselves. There is a reckoning coming quickly which will be very sad, and many of you will find yourselves behind and at a loss in the main business. Do not think that I speak these words to be fashionable; your case requires them all. And therefore yet again, eschew the evil and misery that follows the slighting of such a warning. Do not put it easily and lightly by you for the Lord's sake, for it is hugely above all your greatest concerns in the world to look for death and to provide for it.

The second word shall be to you who through grace began to provide for death, but have become slack, remiss and negligent. Oh, be alarmed and roused up to diligence! Alas, few carefully and conscionably study the art of dying well and in the Lord, and make effort in any tolerable measure as they ought for their appearing before Christ's tribunal. Christians, look to the tract of the best of your lives, how unsuitable it is, and how short of what it should be. There is (alas) much carnality, ruggedness, and untenderness among us, much formality and overliness in duties of worship, much earthly-mindedness, much passion, much pride and vanity. It is a wonder that any who have the faith of their appearing before God, should dare to play such untender pranks, to take such unsuitable latitudes to themselves beside the rule, and to have so gross, so carnal, and so uncircumspect a walk as many of us have. Study more tenderness, Christians, for the Lord's sake; otherwise, though you will get your souls for a prey, and will arrive at last safe at that harbor of rest prepared for the people of God, yet you may, and probably will, have a very unpleasant and uncomfortable voyage, not without several tempests and storms, sometimes threatening utter shipwreck, and find a very strait and difficult entering into the port. When death comes to look you in the face, and when you begin to think of your being so near to an appearance before God, you may be in considerable fear. Now may the Lord Himself, whose Word this is, make it effectual for your edification and advantage through Jesus Christ.

5

When Death Comes Suddenly

"Blessed are the dead which die in the Lord."
Revelation 14:13

It has been an old saying of many that none can be called blessed before their death. Though possibly, in the sense that some heathens took it, it is not sound, yet we who are Christians may say, "If death is not taken in, and if a man is not blessed at his death, he is not blessed at all." And though death, after a very short while's abode in the world, puts men out of time, yet it has a long train of eternal consequences following it. Appearance before God in judgment, and everlasting well or ill being, are not trivial nor light matters; and yet as men close their eyes in time at death, so they may expect the misery or comfort that judgment and eternity will bring along with them. It is the great scope and design of this Scripture to commend to you dying well from the blessedness that accompanies and follows it.

In the last chapter I pressed the practice of some directions how to prepare for death, and shall now speak a little to one question ere I proceed to make any further use of the doctrine.

QUESTION. What shall they do at death who have quite neglected these directions, or not so minded them as they should have done? What shall they do who are brought in a surprise of providence, ere they are aware, near the border and brink of eternity, and who have but few days or rather hours to live?

This is a very important question (and, oh, that folk would study to prevent it by minding the former directions in time), and withal a difficult question to answer solidly and cautiously. For indeed it is not easy to speak to dying persons (whatever many may think of it) who, when they are living, will not hear; and therefore let none make a wrong use of what shall be said to the question. Certainly one wrong use of it would be to delay time and to shift preparing for death till it comes on you. But first put this question seriously to yourselves, how you should live so that you may not have such a question to ask at your death, and that you may eschew the anxiety that such a question has with it at such a time. You will very readily ask the question but heartlessly in sickness who in your health put it off carelessly till death surprises you; and therefore be rather in holy dread of that time when you may scarcely get an hour to think on the business, or may not have liberty for pain and sickness to think on it, or to hear one speak to you about it. This should reasonably stir you up by all suitable means to endeavor to be in a good, fitting, and ready posture before that time comes.

In answer to the question, I shall distinguish unpreparedness for dying in three sorts or kinds of it. There may be three sorts of persons that may be surprised by death in an unprepared condition, and to each of these I shall speak a word.

There is one sort which are absolutely and most sinfully so, who never take any pains at all to be prepared for death till it comes upon them. I may as well speak to stones in the wall as to many of you who are such. A second sort is those who have had some tenderness, but they have fallen slack, negligent, and are out of a good frame. A third sort is such as lack feeling and comfort, and are without clarity of their interest, fearing to die in that condition.

As for the first sort, I say to you, it is no wonder that you slip away securely and fall into the pit of destruction, you who live senselessly and stupidly till death comes upon you; you who never think of death till you and it meet. What can you expect should be spoken to you for your comfort? I shall lay down some grounds to be made use of, even in such a deplorable and desperate-like condition, when folk have quite neglected preparation for death in their health, if such have but one hour to live. Consider:

First, repentance is then possibly attainable. They are within trifling terms with God as long as they are in the land of the living and the sentence has not been passed.

Second, there is no peace to be had with God then but in the same way it is gotten now, that is, by faith in Jesus Christ (which goes along with repentance), and by folks taking themselves to a new way of living, were it but in a sincere resolution. Christ is the way, the truth and the life, and none can come to the Father but by Him (John 14:6). And without faith there is no union with Him. Whoever looks for eternal life must have it through faith in Him.

Third, though a person were to live but one hour, there must be some faith, some repentance, some endeavored clarity of interest, some peace, some holiness though it were but in the bud, so as to speak but a few words to God or to others standing by, as we may see in the thief on the cross. Grace, wherever it comes, even if it but of one hour's age or standing, is still grace, and has the same virtual substantial fruits, or fruits in the bud, that grace of older age and longer standing has.

Fourth, where time is short, there is need that there be some difference from what is ordinary in the death of Christians of longer standing in the state of grace in pursuing these things. In respect of time, to go more speedily through them, that is, to run (as it were) the more swiftly and speedily through repentance and self-examination, fleeing to Christ and the fruits of holiness. If time is short, these would be contracted—not that they would be slighted, but there would be an endeavoring to put them some way together, The Lord says in Matthew 11:12, "The kingdom of heaven suffers violence, and the violent take it by force." There must be a sort of violence even in health in this matter, but more at death; that is, if they do not get all doubts answered, they would at least know that there is an absolute necessity to be in Christ, which must make step over these particular difficulties. The preaching of the moral law in John's time forced people in some way to step over the ceremonies of the Law to Christ; so, by analogy, persons who have been negligent in their life must use the same violence at death. They must have sound repentance and faith, and by these take themselves to Christ speedily. And this speediness is, as I said, to be understood in respect of time. These things fit and qualify a man for Christ, and would be made use of speedily to unite to Him.

A difference would be in respect of the measure, though repentance is in this case shorter; the humiliation would be deeper, though the challenges are shorter; the pangs would be so much more sore; the person would be further down in self-loathing and abhorring. Regeneration and the new birth in such persons born again so very late will readily be with greater pain and sharper pangs, with higher indignation at sin and greater hatred at their own evil ways, than if they had been sooner regenerated.

There would be a difference in respect of eagerness and holy broadenness, which would go beyond the ordinary. It is never good to delay repentance, faith, and holiness, yet folks may come to heaven at a somewhat slower pace in health than when they have put off and delayed these till sickness and death come on them.

Having thus exercised faith and repentance, they would die resolving to be the more in free graces; for if any of Adam's posterity is obliged to God, and bound to be the very humble slaves (if we may speak so) of most sovereignly free grace, most certainly these persons are most singularly so who have been rescued and snatched from death, hell, wrath, and the devil, when he was even ready and about to lay his hands on them, and pull them to the pit with him. So now I say again that none who are in such a condition, nor any of you all, have the least ground of encouragement given from this doctrine to put off or delay faith, repentance, and the study of holiness. Let none therefore take any encouragement, lest they be put to smart for their folly eternally.

As for the second sort, those who have had more tenderness but are backslidden and fallen negligent and out of frame, they are to take the same way. When death puts them in a fright, as it were, and conscience challenges them and stares them in the face, they should renew their repentance and faith in Christ and the fruits of holiness. The more speedily and eagerly they do so, they would be the more humbled, flee more hastily to their city of refuge, come with a more stopped mouth before God, and acknowledge grace to be the freer, and allow it to have the greater glory.

As for the third sort—those who have kept up more tenderness, who would fain have their interest and peace clear, and to this day could never attain to it, or once they had it clear it has grown somewhat dim and dark, and even in a manner worn away again, who grow heartless when death comes and surprises them—to such I would say that believers may die without sensible comfort and still die well; for as sensible comfort is not essentially necessary to folks' justification, so neither is it to their dying in Christ. Folks may die sleeping, in a distemper, or in a spiritual fear, and yet that fear may have faith and love in its bosom. That condition which does not mar a Christian's peace once made with God in their life, and is not so sinful, may also be died in. They may be in the dark and yet die well.

Distinguish between the sense of the joy of the Spirit, and that comfort and joy which a believer may have from God's Word of promise. Believers, both living and dying, may lack the one and have the other. Though they do not have the flowings of the Spirit in sensible comfort and joy, yet they may have solid peace and consolation because they have God's Word of promise to rest on who have fled to Him for their life; and their conscience has an inward testimony that they have denied their own righteousness and taken His— and in this they have peace. How else could a believer possibly lie down in any measure of true quietness under desertion, even for their trial, it may be, more than for their sin? And if we look at David's dying, it is likely that he did not have much comfort; for in those that are called his last words in 2 Samuel 23:5, he takes God's covenant, though he did not so much feel the fruits of it, and rests there as at another anchor.

Therefore, they who are in this condition should with more confidence put themselves in over, upon, and within the compass of the covenant, and make their faith more sure because they lack sensible comfort. It is and will be so with believers at that time, for then they are most out of conceit with their own righteousness, and in a holy fear and solicitude in themselves; for as God allows some to be more untender in their life, and therefore makes them walk without sensible comfort to keep down their vanity and pride, so may He exercise some at death.

Let such so much more trust God and resolve to be more in His debt. They never took shipping thus in death's boat who had cause to fear being drowned and cast away. He is the believers' God and guide not only to death, but even through death. He may go therefore through the valley of the shadow of death and fear no evil (Psalm 23:4).

I come now to add some further uses of the main doctrine to these we made before.

USE 1. Seeing that they are happy who die in the Lord, and miserable who die out of Him, whatever their external condition is, lay less weight on the comforts of this life and be less fearful for the afflictions of it. O believers in Christ, there are, you see, two parts of this use. I will begin with the last one. If happiness is the portion of them who die in the Lord, why should believers, who have clearness of interest and well grounded hopes of dying in the Lord, fear the afflictions, or be much troubled with the ups and downs, of this present life? Though they meet with contempt, reproach, poverty, disgrace, imprisonment, fining, confining, exile, and many challenges, these have an end; death will put a period and close to them all. Their great happiness is not here; it is at the other side of death. All your miseries will soon be at an end, and it is a far more exceeding and eternal weight of glory that is laid up for you. Your time here will not be long; it will be but thirty or forty years for some, ten or twenty years for others. Some will have more or fewer years, and it may be but one year for some of you. And then our blessed Lord Jesus will come and wipe all tears from your eyes, and the comfortless remembrance of these trials, troubles, and tossings shall never enter into heaven with you. It is a shame that believers who have such a hope should be so heartless when they meet with crosses, and walk so discouragedly under them.

Seeing that happiness follows after death, do not lay so much weight on the comforts of this life. What comfort or satisfaction can you have in them at death? And seeing that they can yield you no solid satisfaction then, are you not far much mistaken who bestow your travail and pains on seeking satisfaction among creature comforts, and never labor to enter into His rest? Does any more need to be said to frighten you from this foolish course but to tell you that you leave and forsake the fountain of living waters, and take yourselves to the cisterns that can hold no water, and which will dreadfully beguile and disappoint you? What will riches, pleasures, grandeur, honors, and great places do to you at death? These make but a poor happiness and will soon have an end; and yet there is no lesson in the world that men and women learn less than this. As all creatures say that wisdom is not in them (Job 28), so they all cry with one voice that happiness is not in them. It is not in riches, for they take to themselves wings and flee away; it is not in honor, for man who is in honor and does not understands is like the beast that perishes. He who is high in court today may be hanged tomorrow. Nor is it in pleasures, for the laughter of the fool is madness, and has grief and sadness of heart with it, and even in the midst of it.

USE 2. The second use has two branches also. If happiness follows them who die in the Lord, it calls for a willingness as well as a readiness to die whenever God calls you believers to it. It also serves to condemn a general unwillingness to die even among the people of God. I say, if happiness is in dying in Christ, then they who are on the way to it should be ready, willing, and cheerful to die. It must be an exceedingly great distemper when folks do not hear of death with patience, and it argues strongly that either folk are out of the way, or not clear as to their being in the way. Therefore reflect on your condition: what if God should call any of you this night. Are you willing to die? I believer there is not one among many who could heartily say it. There is scarcely one among many but when death comes they would rather delay it.

I do not say this to condemn the use of lawful means in sickness for recovering health, but to check our great loathness and unwillingness to die, which is such that we would always suspend and put it off. This speaks of little faith regarding the truth that they are happy who die in the Lord; otherwise, if it were solidly believed, folk would be more willing to die and to be with Christ. Yea, there would be a desire to be there. If it were testified to men by persons worthy of credit that there was a good, pleasant, and fertile land to be inhabited in the world, many would move there to make a good fortune in this life. And yet, for all God's testimony (who cannot possibly lie or deceive) of the happiness that follows dying in Christ, yet it is not believed, and therefore few are willing or desirous to go through death to enjoy it. Very few are like Paul, who desired to be dissolved and be with Christ, which is best of all; weakness of faith makes want of willingness to die.

Or else it speaks of great lack of love for Jesus Christ. An unwillingness to die is no little sin, but want of love is greater, when folks prefer being with a husband, a wife, with children or friends, to being with Christ. Oh, love for Christ strangely loosens the heart from these, and makes the soul breathe after being with Him, as that which is best of all.

Or else, third, it speaks much earthly-mindedness, and addictedness to the things of a present world. Hence it is that many carnal and earthly-minded wretches would never desire a better life, or another life than their house and bit of land in quietness, the fellowship of their natural relations and other external enjoyments.

To clear this use further, let me briefly touch on some questions: Is all willingness or desire to die good? And may a Christian sometimes be warrantably unwilling to die?

QUESTION 1. Is all willingness or desire to die good?

ANSWER. Let me distinguish between a sinful and a commendable willingness. First, there is a sinful willingness or desire to die in folks' carnal fits, and it is threefold: There is a desperate willingness, which is when folks do not abide some present horror on their spirits, or some pain of their bodies, or some other very heavy and sharp cross. They will wish to be away, and some in such fits dispatch themselves by their own hands. Judas could not endure the horror of his own conscience, and therefore hung himself. But this is rather an unwillingness to submit to and bear their present lot and case than any willingness to die.

The other two are unique to the godly. The second willingness, then, is when the godly have many crosses that they do not well bear, and are afraid that God is dishonored through their fainting or other miscarriages, or when they see it going ill with God's people and His public work. They cannot do any thing to mend it, and look upon themselves as useless, so would fain be away. Elijah, in 1 Kings 19, prays, "Lord, take away my life," because they had slain his prophets, tore down his altars and he alone was left. He apprehended that they sought to take away his life. But the Lord told him that he was wrong, that He had yet more to do with him, and that matters were not as ill as he thought, for He had reserved seven thousand who had not bowed the knee to Baal. Thus some eminent godly men in an evil time will readily wish to be dead; they do not endure to always be fighting, striving, and contending to help and heal, especially since they think they can do no good. Yet sometimes it is not so much the case of the public—as a fear of being straitened or disappointed in some one or other particular of their own—that is the great ground of their fainting and wishing to be gone, as we may see clearly in eminently godly and faithful Baruch in Jeremiah 45.

The third willingness to die is when a dispensation or affliction reflects sorely on folks' credit, whether they be preachers or more private professors. Either some slip or miscarriage in themselves, or some affront put on them by others, makes them think they will do no more good (though it may be such a thing has come sinfully from others); it may be from want of success in some work committed to them, or some disappointment met with which they may desire to have removed, as we see in Jonah chapter 4, where he desires the Lord to take away his life. Jonah thought of himself as a prophet to be discredited, and he was so headstrong that when the Lord asks him, "Do you do well to be angry, Jonah?" he answered pettishly, "I do well to be angry, even unto death." God then, by the gourd, let him see that it was his particular that too much swayed him, and that he was not right in his desire or his willingness to die.

For the second, the commendable willingness, I shall show you what it is by several properties that it has:

• Right willingness to die is being content to die in prosperity and is submissive to live in adversity. When all things prosper with men, it is a very rare thing to see them willing to die, though in fits of cross dispensations they may seem to be willing. It is to have a submissive mind content to live in adversity, yea, in the midst of greatest troubles that are incumbent or imminent, which is rare. It is to be as Paul was in Philippians 1:23, content to abide or go as God thinks fitting, which is a sweet temper and frame of soul. It is to be willing to live shamed and reproached, and not to be discontented with the down-lookings of honest folks; to go through evil reports as well as good reports, in all things laboring to keep a good conscience, and in prosperity to be content to leave the world and all that is in it when God calls by death—this is a great matter.

• Right willingness flows not so much from a desire to be rid of the troubles of the world as to enjoy Christ and the good which the soul hopes for in and with Him. It is not because either the person's own particular crosses grow, or because confusions, distractions, and contentions in the public increase, that they covet to be out of that life and to be gone; but it is because they long to be with Jesus Christ. We (said Paul in 2 Corinthians 5:4) who are in this tabernacle groan, being burdened. What is the ground? Not that we would be unclothed, but clothed upon; not so much to get the infirmities of the body laid down as to have the glory promised. It is that which sways mainly in the right desire of death or willingness to die.

• Right willingness to die has much desire and endeavor after communion with Christ here, and if it cannot come soon enough (so to speak) to full, immediate, and never to be interrupted communion with Him in the next life, it seeks to make it up by pressing much after the nearest communion with Him in this life. It is an evil token when folk are desirous to die and to be taken away, and yet are found neglecting communion with Christ while they are living. Those who are rightly willing to die will greatly desire and long for fellowship with Christ, and will be much in the delightful contemplation of heaven ere it comes. In their practice tending thitherward, they will be very loath to do anything that may obstruct that so much desired fellowship.

This we may see in David in the Old Testament and in Paul in the New. Oh, how they pray and pant after God. Oh, what pains they take to keep communion with Him! How they labor in all their conversation to so behave that no obstruction from them may be laid in the way of their so much longed for fellowship with Him. Let none then think that it can be a right willingness to die that does not put men to be tender in the study of holiness, and of conformity to Christ in this life. Therefore it is said of Simeon, who was so willing to die, that he was a just and devoted man, waiting for the consolation of Israel; and by him and other such godly persons in his time the temple was frequented night and day.

• That is a right willingness to die that is not by fits, but is continuing and distinct, and goes upon solid grounds. I do not speak of sensible comfort, but of the grounds of faith, of some clearness of interest, and of sweet submission to God's blessed will; for though none needs to wonder much of Simeon's willingness to die when he has Christ in his arms, yet it has this sweet submission to God in it.

QUESTION 2. May even believers be unwilling to die, and is this warrantable?

ANSWER. They may be sometimes unwilling to die, and that not unwarrantably. To clear this I shall speak to two things: to an unwillingness to die upon carnal grounds, and to an unwillingness to die upon good grounds.

First, believers may be unwilling to die from a sinful unpreparedness to die. They may have a loathness to look death in the face through the conscience of some, yea much carnality in their life. Besides that there is in all a natural averseness to dying. Believers may sometimes have their own carnal designs that may make them unwilling, but this is sinful; for where there is a good conscience sprinkled with Christ's blood, solid faith, and clarity about our peace with God, in so far they will make willingness to die.

Second, there is an approved unwillingness that sometimes has been in the saints, as in David and Hezekiah, which is a sweet submission to live rather than a direct desire to live, for other reasons. For if it is a fear about the want of temporal or spiritual things for soul or body, or about anything that relates to God's public work, faith will answer these. But there are two reasons that the saints have gone on, by which they have been induced to this, that made them approved in their unwillingness to die:

(1) The great stroke and influence that their removal might have had on the work of God, as it was in the cases of Hezekiah, Josiah, and Paul. If the former two would have been removed, it would very probably have overturned the work of God, as Paul's removal would have made many sore hearts among Christians.

(2) When their dying in such a case, or under such a dispensation, seems to carry some blot with it on innocent godly persons, or on godliness and the profession of it. If Job had died in his affliction, it would have confirmed his friends in their erroneous opinion. David's dying in the hands of his enemies before he came to the crown would have left some blemish on the faithfulness of God and on the profession of religion, and would have been matter of shame and blushing to the godly. Therefore he says, "For their sakes return Thou on high." So that unwillingness to die that does not flow from respect to a man's self, but from respect to the public work of God, to His glory and other's good, or either of them, is warrantable.

USE 3. The third use also has two branches: Learn

from this doctrine to try and judge what true blessed-ness is: it is to die in the Lord. Learn to think of that as an unhappy thing which is not conducive to this end of dying in the Lord.

First, if you would try your own hearts as to when they are in a spiritual frame, take this as a mark of it: if you really account this to be blessedness. If you were to hear a voice from heaven declaring who is the blessed man, and if you had the Spirit's testimony sealing it, here it is, "Blessed is he who dies in the Lord." It is not they who conquer, overturn, and transfer kingdoms; who obtain many victories and have great success in their achievements and undertakings who are blessed. It is not to be a protector or sole governor of nations that makes a man blessed, but it is to die in the Lord. This is the language of heaven, and that which is laid weight on there, and so should be by you.

Second, lay all the things you can imagine in this world in the balance with this, and they cannot possi-bly weigh equally with it. When all are laid in the bal-ance with dying in the Lord, and with the consequent glory and happiness, they are light as a feather, yea, lighter than vanity, utterly unworthy to be named with these. As there is therefore no happiness in them, so cease to seek it in or from them.

USE 4. A fourth use is of two branches. First, if there is a necessity of dying in the Lord to them who would be happy, there is nothing so forcible to press the study of holiness. Second, nothing is so forcible to scare a person from profanity, which is the great scope of all preaching. I say, consider this doctrine rightly and it will be found to be most powerfully provoking to holi-ness. The reason is because dying well and living well are knit together, and nothing can more demonstrate the absolute necessity of holiness, without which none shall see the Lord. It is as necessary as peace with God and heaven, and whoever they are who do not think so now, whenever they shall be summoned to die, they shall without any doubt find it to be so.

Is there anything that will more frighten a man and deter him from profanity and a carnal walk than this? Gather all that the world can afford, whether of sinful pleasures or of lawful, temporal delights immoderately often used, and suppose that you could come by your very heart's desire and wish in them—what will they all advantage you when death comes? To have so many thousands or hundred thousands of marks, to have so much land or so many houses, will do you no good at death; what will it advantage you to spend your time in pleasure, in the lusts of the flesh, in tippling and drunkenness? And you who are swelled with pride and ambition, and would have all others backing you, and beckoning and bowing to you, what will these profit you when death shall put an end to them all, and make an eternal divorce between you and them; when you must lie down among the dead, and when the worms must cover you?

It is even a wonder (if ought of this kind could be a wonder to our carnal and profane hearts), considering the necessity of dying and of dying in the Lord to all who would die well and happily with the faith and conviction that we generally profess to have of them, that we think so little seriously of death, and of such a death, and are at so little pains in the study of holiness to prepare for it.

I shall therefore in the last place speak a word or two to several sorts of persons, who should be thinking upon and preparing for death, but put it far away from them. Let me speak:

• To them who are young and make a merry life of it, and do nothing but be carnally jovial. Ah, poor wantons, is not death fast approaching? Will it not be upon you ere you be aware, and ere many years go by? Certainly your life will not be eternal, and who knows but your time may be shorter than you dream of? The grave may be as soon filled with you who are younger, healthier, and stronger as with the more aged, sick, and infirmed. What reason then do you have to be so merry and jovial, when your peace is not made sure with God? It is a most remarkable and alarming word that is spoken to you by the Spirit of God in Ecclesiastes 11:9: "Rejoice, O young man in thy youth, and let thy heart cheer thee in the days of thy youth; and walk in the ways of thy heart, in the sight of thine eyes. But know that for all these things God will bring thee into judgment." You may go on, if you will, to your peril, slighting all warnings and admonitions; but be assured that death and judgment are quickly coming, when you will be called to reckon with God not only for every open thing, but for every secret thing, whether good or evil. Therefore be exhorted to review and to cast your eye along your youth, and to consider seriously how it has been spent. See if there is not reason for you to take the exhortation that follows: "Remember now thy Creator in the days of thy youth" (Ecclesiastes 12:1), and to spend some more time in thinking of and preparing for death.

• To them who are exceedingly wise in their own generation; who are very provident for summer and winter, and for all seasons of the year; who can manage their estates very well and put all things in good order for themselves and for their children; who make a convenient life in the world, but do not at all in good earnest mind another life. How many such are there who are very wise for this life, but for the matters of God and their own souls are the starkest fools in the world? Many are like Martha who, though a good woman, was nevertheless much prevailed over by this distemper (albeit it did not reign in her nor obtain dominion over her) as it does over unregenerate persons. They are careful, cumbered, and troubled about many things, and neglect the one thing that is needful. Is it not a wonder that such very rational and wise men should waste all their precious time, except what they spend in eating, drinking, and sleeping, upon the things of a present life, and not allow so much as one hour of all the week to think seriously on their souls and of death? I appeal to your own consciences if this is reasonable, and a practice worthy of rational men who have immortal souls that are capable of eternal happiness and misery. Is your time not spent on these things which are but vanity, and which at death will do you no good or profit you, and concerning which you will then be made to cry? What profit have we of these things whereof we are now ashamed?

• To such as are frequent in their attendance on public ordinances, and in the use of other commanded means, and yet never thought or believed their souls to be in hazard, nor in good earnest prepared themselves for dying. Oh, think yet upon your hazard, for that is the first spring of making ready for the remedy! Oh, seek grace to examine yourselves, to believe in Christ, to repent, and to live as becomes them who profess themselves to be dying persons! It is really both strange and wonderful how it comes to pass that you can so often hear and yet give no obedience to what ye hear. Do you or can you think that it is religion enough to hear? Has not the Scripture said in James 1 that it is not the hearer, but the doer of the Word who is blessed in his deed or doing? I beseech you, therefore, "be ye doers of the Word and not hearers only, deceiving your own souls," or, as the word is, "deluding and playing the sophist with your own souls."

• To them who have greater parts and abilities, and

higher places and power than others, and have withal more opportunities to be preparing for death; who are masters of families and can command their children and servants to read the Scripture, to fast and pray, and seek God; and who know from the Word what is right and what is wrong, what is duty and what is sin, and yet are so very little in the practice of these directions in order to their preparation for death. Consider, I entreat you, what your knowledge, parts, places, and power will do to you or advantage you when you are dying, if there is no faith and love, and the fruits of both in practice. It is really a wonder that so many men should have light in and conviction of these things, and yet should so dally with their light and conviction and not endeavor to make them practical.

• To them who are aged and have one foot, as it were, in the grave; who are sixty or seventy years old, and yet are, even when so far on in years, as secure and negligent in preparing for death as if it were a hundred years from them. Consider what you are doing! Age (alas) and years do not necessarily bring along with them more tenderness in soul concerns, for we see in experience oftentimes that the more aged men are, the more stocked they are in ignorance and senselessness. Certainly, if this speaks to anyone, it speaks to you who should in a manner be carrying your death clothes around with you, and be exemplary to others in preparing for death.

• To those who are in a poor, mean, and low condition in the world; for all are not rich and wealthy, nor do all have a plentiful outward condition. Many can scarcely get their families maintained, and yet even but few of such (which is a wonder) are seriously seeking after heaven, and preparing for the dying in the Lord that leads to it. The rich have a temptation that you do not have. If any in the world should seek after heaven it should be you who are poor; and yet how many of you will be miserable not only here, but also eternally hereafter, ere you take yourselves to the way of holiness? If you were wise, as you ought to be, you would bless God that ever this gospel came among you and was preached to the poor, which has happiness and everlasting riches in the bosom of it to all who will embrace it. Oh, take this word to you, both poor and rich! You will all most certainly lie down in the grave, but this will be the difference: you will either die happy or accursed as you die in Christ or out of Him.

Finally, I must speak to them who have some acquaintance with God, and some conviction of the futility and great deficiency of their endeavors in preparing for death, for their both humbling and further upstirring to diligence, that there is among us both little rousing of ourselves, little hastening to the coming of the day of God, and little going out to meet the bridegroom. Alas, though we are drawing nearer to death daily, yet few of us are waiting for and hastening unto the coming of Christ and of the day of God.

I shall close all with this one word, it may be that many of us shall taste death before we hear so much spoken of it. Take it therefore as an advertisement and call from heaven to mind more that which is so much forgotten, and yet so necessary to be always remembered, even to live so as we may die in the Lord Christ, and so be eternally and unspeakably blessed.

6

Death Is a Suitable Subject for Meditation

"Blessed are the dead which die in the Lord."
Revelation 14:13

Although I have already spoken at greater length on
these words than at first I intended, yet something re-
mains that is useful, and which seems to be the main
scope of the words. Therefore I shall insist a little further. The way that I gather what I am to say is by considering the Spirit's purpose and design in this place,
which comes in very remarkably, having no particular
dependence (it would seem) on the former words, nor
connection with what follows. What can be the reason
that, between the denunciation of judgment before and
the prophecies of judgment that follow, there is such
an interruption and breaking off from the series of the
history made? "I heard a voice saying to me, 'Write,
"Blessed are the dead which die in the Lord from
henceforth." ' " There must surely be some reason.

I shall offer these two reasons that point especially
at the scope of the Spirit of God and are insinuated in
the words that will be the grounds of two doctrines.
The first reason is that when the Lord is speaking of
sad things to come upon His church, and of judgments
to come upon the enemies thereof, He casts this in as a
ground of profitable meditation to His people at such a
time; so that, whether we look to judgments to come on
enemies, or at the trials and temptations His own
people are to meet with, this is cast in seasonably as a
practical lesson, which is plain in itself and profitable

to them. A second reason is that God, by such a word, when death should be frequent and trouble and confusion should grow, may comfort and encourage His people so that death may not be bitter nor terrible to them, since the Lord puts this motto on men's dying in Him in the darkest and saddest times: they are blessed.

These two being the scope, the one to prepare them for dying and the other to comfort them against dying, they yield us two useful points of doctrine:

DOCTRINE 1. Death, and the happiness of them that die in the Lord, is a suitable and profitable subject of the meditation of God's people, especially in times of difficulty and trouble.

This is clearly implied in the words. Certainly the Spirit who is so wise, and who most opportunely times and tries things for the good of His people, would not so abruptly have broken in on this purpose at this time if it were not very pertinent and suitable to such a time. There is not in all of Scripture such a remarkable diversion from the series of history, having such a word prefixed to it, and such a word affixed and subjoined to it as this. This is, no doubt, to stir up God's people who have this book to read, when they come to this memorable passage, to think and consider it the more seriously.

To clear the doctrine more generally, we find that these who have been most holy have been most frequent in the thoughts and meditation of death. So David prayed in Psalm 39, "Lord, make me to know mine end, and the number of my days, that I may know how frail I am." Moses prayed, "So teach us to number our days, that we may apply our hearts to wisdom" (Psalm 90:12). Numbering our days is seriously thinking and meditating on our approaching death. We may here also look on the example of our blessed Lord Jesus Christ in Luke 9:31, who speaks at His transfiguration on the mount with Moses and Elijah of His decease, which He was to accomplish at Jerusalem; for though there was something peculiar in His death, yet His speaking of it and preparing for it belongs as a common duty to us, and should be a pattern to us. Oh, how Solomon commends meditating on death (Ecclesiastes 7:2; 11:8–9, and chapter 12 throughout)!

But for further and more particular clearing of this doctrine, I shall speak a little to these three things contained in it: What is meant when we say that death is a suitable subject of meditation? What profit or advantage comes to the people of God by it? And why do we say it is especially profitable and advantageous to be thought upon in an evil time?

1. When we speak of death as a suitable subject of meditation, it is not to be strictly taken as contradistinguished from other things that precede, accompany, and follow death. But, first, we take in the thoughts of the certainty of dying, and the uncertainty of its time and other circumstances as to us. It is then to think on death as the way of all flesh, as that which no man can get a discharge from, and of the uncertainty of the time and manner of it, how sudden and surprising it may be. Second, when we speak of the meditation of death, we take in all that accompanies it, the pain and outward diseases whereby men are made unable to do any profitable work in their generation, as well as all the challenges, convictions, temptations, terrors, and anxieties that accompany death, and the estimation of things that we see dying men to have. All these should be taken in as a part of this meditation. Third, when I speak of meditating on death, I do not mean that it should only be meditated on as a natural thing after the fall of man, but we should consider and distinguish it in its several kinds as its dying in sin and dying in the Lord, the first and second death. We should look

upon death on the one hand as an effect of the curse, and on the other hand as being sweetened with God's love, and as an entry into happiness. We should add to this the causes of the one and of the other, what it is that makes death miserable to one and happy (or the entry to happiness) to another. Fourth, when we speak of thinking on death, we should take in the effects and consequences of death, our appearing before God, judgment, and eternity, that are at the back of death; entering into an unchangeable estate of well or ill being, meeting with a sentence that is irrevocable, the eternal happiness of them who die in Christ, the eternal misery of them who die in sin, perfection of joy, and extremity of sorrow forever, which men and angels are not able to conceive, and are far less able to express.

And when we speak of meditation on death, we say it is a suitable subject to be thinking often and frequently on all these, not only at more solemn and set times, but even in the midst of our callings and employments, in the midst of our joy, and of our grief and sadness; to be taking some serious looks at this day that will put an end to all these in the way before spoken of. In your youth, consider that this day of darkness is coming. And in old age especially, when the shadow of death sits down on the eyelids and the strong men begin to bow themselves, think on these things.

2. To commend this duty to you all, consider what advantage flows from it. Though I spoke of meditation in general at another occasion, and hinted somewhat at meditation on death, yet it is so frequently spoken of in the Scriptures, and so profitable to believers, that I shall speak a little to some advantages that will commend the expedience of the duty, as well as the necessity of it to you.

First, much of the improvement of the great truths I have been speaking of to you depends on your meditation on death, and these things that go before, accompany, and follow after it. It is impossible to know aright, and to believe how great a task and work it is to die well, and what is the happiness of them who die so, if we are not taking pains to be cleared and confirmed in it by Scripture. and by meditating on it. Folks take but a glance at it, but do not stay to look on the quarrel and controversy that is between God and them. Neither do they consider seriously what is at the back of death, and therefore it surprises them when it comes. But that man can speak of death boldly and advisedly who has been acquainting himself with it beforehand.

Second, nothing more heightens the estimation of God and Christ than the thoughts of death. These thoughts brings folks closer and nearer to His bar, and make them look on Him as Judge; they make them consider their futility, baseness, and vileness on the one hand, and the greatness of the majesty of God upon the other. Oh, how sublimely David and Job speak of God! In one word they talk of the grave, and of the cover of worms there, and in the other word they highly exalt the majesty and greatness of God. Meditation on death brings the thoughts of what God is, and of what we are, very near to us, and represents to us beforehand what He will be found to be at and after death, and what we will be then. On the contrary, it is given as a root of our despising God when men put the evil day far away, as no doubt a root of reverence and respect to God is serious meditation on death.

Third, if you look at believers conversing with others who have grace, or that abound in corruption, we find it exceedingly needful, useful, and advantageous to carry along the thoughts of death. It would make Christians walk lovingly and edifyingly with others, loath to do wrong; more patient when suffering wrongs, more able to forgive, and more ready to forget wrongs. Our carnal humors would not get their way if the thoughts of dying were suitably entertained; and half an hour's discourse, together with the impression of it on us, through God's blessing, would edify and profit us mutually more than many days meeting without it could do.

Fourth, in reference to a man's self, meditation on death is a most quieting and spirit-sobering thing. It stays the mind, diverts it from vanities, and removes them from being the object of his pursuit. Nay, in some way it crucifies Him to them. Hence it is that men are seldom or never in a more sober and a better frame than when they are seriously apprehensive of death. When men are sick, or are in danger at sea or on land, they will readily be in another frame than ordinarily they are in. And when the danger is gone, that impression wears easily off. But were we more in meditation on death, this frame might be more constant and lasting.

More particularly, this meditation on death contributes, through God's blessing, to rectify a man's judgment that, by original sin, is darkened, and accounts ill good and good ill. The thoughts of death make a man wise, discreet, and condescending. While men have good health, and are without these thoughts, they will rather wound their conscience than their credit; to get their barns full and all going well with them in the world, wholly takes them up. But serious thoughts of death makes them wise to discern and judge things. Therefore Moses joined these two together, thinking on death and applying the heart to wisdom in Psalm 90.

When folks do not think on death, they are encumbered with many things. They run to cisterns and turn their back on the fountain; whereas serious pondering on death lets the vanity and emptiness of these things be seen. How many we see daily, when dying, counting little of these things they thought much of before, and calling and accounting themselves fools who allowed themselves to be so carried away with them. God's Spirit calls them fools who make such a choice.

As it enlightens the judgment, so it orders the affections and rules the passions. Therefore, when Solomon speaks to the young man who will be tried with no bands, he ironically bade him rejoice and laugh on, but withal willed him to remember that, for all these things, he will come to judgment. Meditating on death and judgment would say of laughter, "You are mad," and of mirth, "What are you doing?" It would make men look on them as vanity, folly, and madness. And these thoughts especially would become folks in prosperity, and in their youth when their humors are more high bended and light. Meditation on death is a notable bridle to lightness.

This is exceedingly profitable to advance mortification, to bring us out of the entanglements of the world, and to help us with singleness and deniedness in following Christ. "You fool," says death, "this night your soul may be taken from you. And whose then shall all these things be?" It makes men's carousing and good fellowship (as they call it) tasteless. In that case, conscience would say, "What if you die drunk, or with the cup in your hand?" This meditation would make a man care little for the world, riches, pleasures, or honor. It would make all grow very unsavory.

In a word, it mortifies these three things, which are the world's trinity: pride, covetousness, and carnal lusts. It mortifies pride, as we may see in David, who says in Psalm 39, "Lord, teach me to know my end and the measure of my days, that I may know how frail I am." Job says of corruption that it is his mother, and that the worms are his sisters. Pride makes us say, "Dust I am, and to the dust I shall return."

Meditating on death would mortify covetousness, for meditating on death wrings the heart from the things of the world, and gives a man other thoughts to think on. How many, when death approaches, are forced to say that they have encumbered themselves with the world, and it has beguiled them.

It mortifies carnal pleasures, for what can vain fleshly lusts do to men who are dying? For as merry as they are now, these thoughts say, they must appear within a little while before God in judgment. And if this is not a bridle to these lusts, I do not know what will be a bridle.

Meditating on death stirs a man up to the diligent exercise of all duties, and to going about them soberly and seriously. One sermon or prayer after serious meditation on death would have more weight, and would be waited on with more advantage, than many others without it. It puts us to humiliation, self-examination, and self-searching; it furthers the exercise of the fear of God, and brings the soul to stand in awe of Him, before whom it is to appear shortly. It furthers repentance and prayer (Job 41:25). Because of breakings they purify themselves; they make themselves ready for death by repentance, prayer, and offering sacrifices, even these heathens in the ship with Jonah. And if meditating on death puts profane men to a form of religion, how much more will it put believers to be serious and spiritual in the exercise of these duties and the practice of religion? And if God gives them time and seriousness at dying, their prayers will be more useful and fervent at that time than before.

It is exceeding profitable to work kindly submission to cross-dispensations, and to make folks go softly under them. What will a man care, who is taken up with meditating on death, if he forfeits his estate or sees his house burned, or his land wasted? He knows that death will put an end to all these things.

As it fits for all duties and restrains from all vices, so it exceedingly prepares for death itself, which is the great scope. Solomon described sickness and old age in Ecclesiastes 12 as making the young man ready for death ere it comes. And if there were no other advantage from meditating on death, this is no small one: not to be surprised by it. Yea, in some way it also mitigates the bitterness of death, so that it is not as terrible to them who have been thinking seriously on it as it is to others who have never made it the subject of their meditation. And what wonder is it to see many who are either mightily terrified or very stupid at death, since they never studied the lesson of dying before it came on them?

3. Meditating on death is especially advantageous in evil times. This seems to be the very scope of the words, and the godly such as David and others have thought it so. I do not say that meditating on death is especially profitable and advantageous in ill times, as if it were not to be thought on in times of prosperity and peace, but that it is exceedingly necessary and singularly profitable in an evil time. The great necessity and advantage of this arises from three things that accompany an evil time:

• Many snares and temptations. In an ill time, flesh and blood are ready to postpone a good conscience and prefer self-preservation. But living in the meditation of death guards against that. If the temptation say, "Man, spare or save yourself," the soul that is thinking on death will say, "I may soon lose my good conscience by yielding to such a thing for self-preservation, and yet I may not live a year after it. And though I should live twenty, yet shall I be brought to account for it. Therefore, I will rather hazard the loss of anything, yea of life itself, than to wound or make shipwreck of my conscience by provoking God." Hence the apostle tells us in 2 Corinthians 5 that he was not swayed with the outward things.

• Carnal sorrow, fainting, perplexity, and discouragement. Meditating on death mitigates these. It says that these things, or any other thing the godly can suffer, are not eternal. It sweetens our grief and diverts the mind from carnal thoughts to that which is more profitable; it eases the mind, allays the storms, and calms the confusions that outward difficulties and troubles raise and awaken in it; it gives a profitable use of sad things.

• Much confusion and distraction. What is down, we think should be up, and what is up, we think should be down. Our minds are ready to stagger, and reel to and fro like a drunken man, because of these confusions; but the thoughts of death stay the mind, and say that death ere long will bring all these things to an end, or else an end to us, and will bring them all to be recognized and judged over again. To this purpose compare Ecclesiastes 3:16–17, where Solomon says, "I saw the place of judgment, that wickedness was there, and the place of righteousness, that iniquity was there." And what comforted him against this? "I said in my heart, God will judge the righteous and the wicked; for there is a time there for every purpose and for every work." Oftentimes there is not a season for things here, but at death there is a season for everything. All sentences that have been wrongly passed here will be reduced there. The consideration of this stays his heart and comforts him.

Application

USE OF EXHORTATION. Let all that has been said commend this excellent-though-much-slighted duty, not only meditation in general, but meditation in particular on the subject of death. Folks have often as little mind of this duty as if it were not in the Word of God, and yet it is frequently called for there. It is especially needed in a generation wherein there is so much confusion, turning of things upside down and reeling to and fro; so many snares and so many grounds of grief and sorrow; when so many are carnally weighted and dejected, and so many are declining and going wrong. I think that this text relates to this time of the world, the time of God's beginning to execute His judgments on antichrist before the full harvest and vintage comes. And therefore I would speak to this use a little more particularly because it is very useful, and is a notable means to make you go profitably about the practice of all that I have spoken to this purpose; for it puts us in mind of these directions for right living in order to dying, and it holds us to them. Without minding death, there can be no minding of these directions; for those who do not mind the end can never mind the mean.

Because it is this useful, I shall therefore speak a little on some directions or rules, showing how you should think on death, and then give some helps and means thereto.

DIRECTION 1. Be particular in your meditation. Apply it to yourself in particular. It is not enough to take for granted that death is common to all. So does Job in chapter 30:23: "I know that Thou shalt bring me to death." So does David in Psalm 39:4: "Lord, teach me to know mine end and the number of my days, how frail I am." Go through all the concomitants of death;

consider what your case at death may be, what your challenges, temptations, and thoughts will; and what will be the effects and consequences of death to you, when you must behold and face your Judge.

DIRECTION 2. Cast a reflexive look on yourselves and your own way in meditation. When you consider what prepares one to die well, look back and see if such a preparation is in you; consider how your way suits with that which the Scripture holds out to be the way, if such a challenge may meet you at death, and what course is taken with it to answer or prevent it. This was Job's way (chapter 31), where he tells us that he dared not slight the cause of his manservant or maidservant when they contended with him; for then he would not have had a good answer to his judge. And if he had done otherwise, it would have marred his boldness.

DIRECTION 3. Labor to have your affections moved in your meditations on death; This is a chief end of meditation; otherwise we will but run to and fro, and rove up and down to inform the judgment, and carry the thoughts of death as a common place along with us, but will get no good from it. The special thing is to have something come from it that may melt the heart, as it was with David in Psalm 77, "I thought on God and was troubled." And Psalm 63:5, "My soul shall be filled as with marrow and fatness." There is something like this in meditating on death; it affects the heart with terror when the soul thinks on dying without clarity of interest. It affects the heart with comfort and joy when the soul is clear in its interest; to think on dying in Christ so as thereby to be advanced a step nearer unto it, and to drink in what we have been thinking upon, that is the truly profitable thinking on such a thing. That meditation which does not affect the heart is like chewing meat that is immediately spit out again and not swallowed and digested. It is looking only on what is profitable without making any use of it. Such, I say, is all our preaching, hearing, speaking, and thinking of death when they do not affect the heart.

DIRECTION 4. Study to be practical in your meditation, that is, to have it tend to some profitable use in your practice as its end. When you find such a thing to be wrong, immediately set about to amend it. When you find something spiritually profitable, resolutely go about it and use all means to attain it.

DIRECTION 5. Seek to be much in prayer to God, and in dependence on Him for direction in this particular. Go about meditation on death as a duty commanded by God, with prayer to Him and with dependence on Him for His assistance and His blessing on it. Many do not look on the meditation of death in particular as a peculiar duty, and therefore it is so much slighted.

When I commend it to you as a duty, I mean these three things:

First, look upon it as required of God, and as being useful and profitable as well as any other duty.

Second, go about it as in His presence. Ordinarily, folks take a greater latitude in meditation than in prayer, but ye should remember and consider that He is witness to your meditation as well as to your prayers, that He is the greater subject of it, that it is laid on by His command, that suitable meditation is and must be wrought by His Spirit, and that you will and must count on Him for your wanderings in it as well as in prayer.

Third, take time for it, and purpose to do it when perhaps you might have something to do that is not necessary. By prayer, seek God's guidance in this particular duty as well as in any other duty. This Moses does in Psalm 90:12: "Teach us to number our days." Do not be frightened by the apprehended difficulty of it, for as meditation in general is hard and difficult, so the particular meditation of death is a subject that we are naturally very averse from. Therefore David prayed in Psalm 39:4, "Lord, teach me to know mine end." And indeed, a more frequent and habitual exercise and practice of it would, through God's blessing, make it more easy.

Now, as I promised, because there is difficulty in this duty, as I have just now hinted, I shall therefore point out a few helps to it. There is nothing we have more motives to, nor more memorandums of (to say so), than of this; therefore take these helps:

HELP 1. Consider seriously the frequent deaths and burials among you every day, whereof you are witnesses, and at which you are present, possibly of several younger, healthier, and stronger persons than yourselves, and of whom it might have been thought not many days since they would have outlived you. Then reflect upon yourselves, and see if you are prepared for death when you are in your houses or going in the streets, and hear the bell giving notice of the death of such and such persons, or see the corpses carried forth to their burial place—think on these things, for they are helpful. Therefore Solomon says, "Better is the day of death than of one's birth." And he gives the reason: "for the living will lay it to heart," that is, the living *should* lay it to heart.

HELP 2. Look unto and consider well your own infirmities, sickness, and diseases of one kind or another. There are none but have the seed of fewer or of more diseases in them, besides fits of sickness that befall them now and then. And what is the language of all these but this? "Dust thou art, and to dust shalt thou return." When folks have in their bodies the beginnings of rottenness or a gangrene, those will spread. You would hear all these infirmities, diseases, and distempers crying aloud that you will and must die; for these cry to you every day. A man once appointed someone to cry at his door every morning, "You are mortal!"

HELP 3. Consider the extraordinary events that befall many men and women. Some are suddenly struck down with palsies; some fall down and never rise; some go abroad and never return; some are struck with fury and madness—and are any of us exempt from any of these?

HELP 4. I commend to you frequent reading of and meditating on those Scriptures that speak of death, and other books that treat the subject, those which set forth most lively the shortness of man's life. Often read of the death of the saints. Many are rather taken up with reading vain romances or stories that are unprofitable in comparison of this; and others are, it may be, taken up with mysterious, dark, doubtful, and little edifying questions and debates.

HELP 5. Think seriously on the names that death gets in Scripture, and the comparisons whereby it is there held forth; for there are not many things that we can readily mention or meet with which may not serve to put us in mind of dying. Do men put off their clothes? Death is compared to that in 2 Corinthians 5. Do we lie down in our beds to take rest? Death is also compared to that in Isaiah 57:2, where the prophet says that the righteous shall "enter into peace, they shall rest in their beds." To the same purpose death is compared to a sleep: "One generation goes and another comes, and every one sleeps their sleep" (Psalm 76:5). If you would reflect when you are going to bed and consider what posture you are lying down in, and from this think with yourselves what is out of order, how you may be suitably affected with it, and rise up in the morning with a resolution to practice accordingly—it would be a profitable meditation. Death is also called "the way of all flesh," and can we reckon our age or number our years without it at least putting us in mind of the death that is fast coming? Yea, can we so much as breathe (which is one of the most ordinary things) without it putting us in mind of death? "Thou takest away their breath; they die and return to their dust," says Psalm 104:29. If there were but a stop put to this continual breathing of ours, then our life would be quickly found to be but as a vapor that goes up and does not return again, that appears but for a little time and then vanishes away, as James 4:14 says. So we do not lack sufficient occasions to put and keep us in mind of death. But, alas, we lack heart and affection to the thing, and spiritual-mindedness to make use of these occasions. I leave it with you not only as a duty, but as a very profitable duty, to meditate more on death and to make use of these and the like means to help you to it, and the Lord Himself bless them to you.

USE OF REPROOF AND CONVICTION. Oh, what ground of reproof and challenge this brings along with it! Were this the very time of our going to die, and of our appearance before our Judge, how many of us could say that we have made conscience of thinking on our last end? So the Lord may expostulate with us as He did with His people of old in Deuteronomy 32, as with a foolish and unwise people: "Oh, that they were wise! Oh, that they understood this, that they would consider their latter end!" Many may sadly say that they scarcely ever reckoned it among their duties, nor the neglect of it among their sins and grounds of challenge. And I fear, which is yet worse and more sad, that it may be said of many that they do not resolve to rank and place it among their duties. But if you will not be prevailed upon to make it and mind it as your duty, be assured that it shall be your sin, and you shall have it for your challenge. What? Do you not have the command of God enjoining it? Does not the saints practicing it so much hold some weight with you? The plainness of the duty will make your guilt the greater, and you the more inexcusable, in your neglecting it. There are none of us but may go home with many challenges for being so entangled with the things of the world, and for the levity, unstayedness, insobriety, and carnalness of our spirits, which make us think so little and speak so little of dying. And if any thoughts of it occur now and then to our minds, they do not sink in; they do not affect us; and they do not leave suitable impressions. If you would examine it seriously, you would find the fruit of it to be further holiness. It would sober and compose you, and fit you for anything that may be coming in an ill time; for doing and for suffering as you may be called to it, and for death itself. May God Himself give you the grace to endeavor it, so that you may find the blessed fruit and advantage of it.

7

The Believer's Encouragement in Death

"Blessed are the dead which die in the Lord."
Revelation 14:13

Since sin entered into the world, death has been one of the most terrible things that the children of men have to meet with, even the most terrible of all terrible things. Indeed, it is no wonder that they who do not know of another and better life to come, nor of the way how to come at it, esteem so of it. It is called by Job 18:14 "the king of terrors." All other terrors are petty and inconsiderable in respect of this; and it is one of the believing Christian's great privileges that he is armed for death, and that death is disarmed regarding him. Death becomes a kind friend to the believer, and the terror of it is taken away; and that which the stoutest people dare not, do not, composedly look in the face (though in a fit of manliness, as they call it, or rather of desperateness indeed, some will endeavor to brave it out against death and to bear down the terror of it), the true Christian, only through faith in Christ, is a victor over this enemy death.

The scope of these words in our text is that the Lord knows how in these calamities and troubles that were coming death would be frequent, and that many of the bodies of His saints would go among the rest, though their death is very precious in His sight. He knows also how despicable their death will be in the eyes of the profane world, and that they would be accounted as the only wise and happy men who could best shift suffering for Christ and for His truth. And knowing withal how tempting this would be unto them, He permits this seasonable and sweet word of comfort, "Blessed are the dead which die in the Lord." It is as if He has said, "Do not let believers in Christ think much of death; it will not mar their happiness, but shall rather further and hasten it." So that these words are given to strengthen and comfort the godly against such an evil time.

From this ground I propose this second doctrine:

DOCTRINE. God has fully furnished the believer in Him with comfort and encouragement against the terribleness of death, so that, though death is terrible in itself, yet the believer has good and sufficient ground of encouragement against it, and may quietly and comfortably die when God calls him, wherever and however it shall be. There is nothing in death that he needs to fear. The Word of God has given him notable grounds of comfort and encouragement to bear him through it most heartsomely, and in the faith of that Word he should walk confidently and comfortably through the valley of the shadow of death and fear no ill.

There are two things in this doctrine to much the same purpose: First, the Lord allows the believer to be comforted in his death, and therefore He has allowed him grounds of strong consolation. Second, the believer who has these grounds should make use of them to bear him cheerfully and comfortably through death. So the Lord, speaking of death and judgment in Luke 21:28, says to and commands believers in Him, "When ye shall see these things come to pass, then look up and lift up your heads; for the day of your redemption draweth nigh." Beside this one, there are many other commands that are frequent in the Scriptures to this purpose. And how many of the saints, resting on these grounds, have died most willingly, pleasantly, comfortably, and joyfully?

Take for instance old Simeon, who sweetly says in Luke 2, "Now lettest Thou Thy servant depart in peace." He begs to be gone. And if you look at Paul, how earnestly he longs for his pass and demission, and how heartily he welcomes the thoughts of it in Philippians 1:21.

To clear the doctrine a little, I shall speak somewhat to two things: What the things are that ordinarily make death terrible, and what the grounds of comfort and refreshment, or the refreshing considerations that believers have in the way of grace against these grounds of terror, are. The latter will be found far greater than the former. Only take this word of caution or warning: I do not speak of death so as if it were comfortable to die simply, or as if it were so to all; no, not so, for it is terrible to all them who die in sin and out of Christ. But to them who believe in Him, and take His own way to this blessed end of dying in Him, to all them and to them only, is death comfortable and refreshing, and to none others.

1. As to these things that make death terrible and so much to be feared, they are especially these five:

(1) There is something natural in death that makes it terrible, and that is the dissolution of that in time, close, and strait union which is between the soul and the body. The separation of these two great intimates, being contrary to nature, cannot but be abhorrent and terrible to it. And since death, in its large extent, is a part and fruit of the curse, and a bitter fruit of man's departure from God, it is no wonder it is terrible.

(2) There is something in death that is penal. As it is the wages of sin, it has challenges flowing from the law with it, which speak to the conscience. This is the fruit of sin, and has a right with it to dominion over the sinner flowing from the breach of the Law of God. Were there nothing more than this in death, it might

make it terrible to all. Hence it is said in 1 Corinthians
15:56 that the sting of death is sin, because it would be
nothing to die if there were no challenge for sin in it.
And the strength of sin is the Law, because the Law
curses "everyone that continueth not in all things that
are written in it to do them" (Galatians 3:10). So by this
means death has dominion over all, and brings all in
their natural condition under wrath.

(3) There is something that is accidental (if I
may so speak) in death, and that is the greatness and
grievousness of pain that ordinarily takes hold of men
and women when death, as a king of terrors, draws
near. Sometimes other circumstances concur to make
it terrible, namely, that it comes at such a time very sur-
prisingly; that it comes by such a sort of sickness that
may be loathsome and sometimes thought of as shame-
ful; that it tries the person in such a place and among
such a company, and perhaps at a distance from all
friends and familiars.

(4) There is something unfamiliar and strange
in death that makes it terrible. The man who is now dying never died before, and none can tell him fully what
and how great a thing it is to lay down his life. This is a
thing which he never experienced before; for his
thoughts, affections, delights, desires, and designs are
all much changed and altered from what they were.
Yea, that wherein he had pleasure is now possibly his
bane and torment; his thoughts of the world are quite
another thing than they were before. It is no wonder
then that folks are scared and are very fearful to adventure on a voyage whereof none can give them a particular and exact account as having sailed it before them,
with which they themselves have never been acquainted, and which has such terrible effects, especially
where faith in Christ is lacking.

(5) That which accompanies and follows death

makes it terrible. If a person were simply to return to dust as a beast does, it would be terrible enough; but to have an immortal soul that must appear before the tribunal of the great God, and must go through the hands of His holy and severe justice, where the least sin will draw damnation, and where the sentence that is once past is never to be revoked—oh, what a concerning and terrible thing that is! And however little men think of it while they are healthy, yet it has a broad look at death. Nay, if you will consider men as men, much more as having some light of the gospel, you would think it a matter of admiration that the serious thoughts of what follows after death does not put them quite beside themselves, and frighten them out of their wits. However, to die carelessly and without satisfaction, without an interest in Christ, is doubtless a most terrible thing.

2. If you look to the allowance that believers have, and to their grounds of comfort against these things that are terrible in death, you will see them to be far greater and stronger than they are terrible. Consider the grounds of the believer's peace and comfort in dying, and the fruits that flow from these grounds, which are exceedingly refreshing and encouraging, and which you would carefully gather and lay up against the time of dying, and take such a way of living as you may have right to them when you come to die.

For the grounds of a believer's peace and comfort, consider first God's over-ruling providence in the least circumstance that concerns a believer's death. "Precious in the sight of the Lord is the death of His saints" (Psalm 116:15). He looks to their death as a matter of special concern. The time, the sickness, the kind of death, whether violent or natural, a lingering or sudden death, are all determined and concluded with Him. David said, "Thou art my God; my times are in Thy hand. Deliver me from the hand of mine enemies" (Psalm 31:15). His interest in God sweetened all to him, and it also comforted him against the persecution of enemies. It was not in men's hands to put an end to his life when they pleased, but in God's.

Second, consider our Lord Jesus's special commission, with reference to death, as He is the Mediator whom God has furnished with all power in heaven and earth. Therefore, when John is afraid to die in Revelation 1:18, Christ laid His hand on him and said, "Fear not, I have the keys of hell and of death." The godly need not be surprised with it, as if it could seize or take hold of them without commission; for death does not have the keys in itself, but Christ bears them all. The world cannot take the bodily life of a saint from him till Christ grants a commission for that effect: Is it not then very comfortable to be in such a blessed estate where Christ orders and commands all? Most certainly it is.

Third, consider our Lord's satisfaction and death. This one has many grounds of comfort in it. He died and was laid in the grave, hence He has satisfied the Law and taken away the curse. 2 Corinthians 5:21: "He was made sin for us who knew no sin; that we might be made the righteousness of God in Him." "Christ hath redeemed us from the curse of the law, being made a curse for us" (Galatians 3:13). "Blotting out the handwriting of ordinances that was against us, and that was contrary to us, taking it out of the way and nailing it to His cross, and having spoiled principalities and powers, He made a show of them openly, triumphing over them in it" (Colossians 2:14–15). His death is our victory over death. He disarmed the devil by His dying, and became the death of death, as it is in Hosea 13:14: "O death, I will be thy plague. O grave, I will be thy destruction." By laying in the grave, He has sweetened it to believers so that they need not fear lying where He lay.

His resurrection completes the consolation; it shows that death is His captive, that it did not prevail over Him, but that He prevailed over it and spoiled it of its power. So believers may now sweetly sing, "O death, where is thy sting? O grave, where is thy victory? Thanks be to God, who hath given us the victory through Christ's resurrection! He has satisfied for us and in our place!" This is the ground of the apostle's triumph in Romans 8:33: "Who shall lay anything to the charge of God's elect? It is God that justifies, who shall condemn? It is Christ that died, yea, rather that is risen again."

Let the law, justice, the devil, and sin come forth; they have no just ground of challenge or plea against the believer for the debt is paid. Christ is dead and risen, and has gotten a discharge: this is the foundation of a believer's comfort. Consider that Christ died to prevent all right in any party or person to challenge him.

His intercession yet further completes the consolation, for He has not left the believer to die alone nor to live alone; but the benefits of His purchase are made forthcoming for him, according to His prayer in John 17:24 (and He is the same now in heaven that He was on earth), where He says, "Father, I will that these whom Thou hast given me be with Me where I am, that they may behold My glory." The sum of His intercession is to get believers made conquerors, and it is not fully satisfied till they are completely so. This is a great ground of comfort, that when the believer cannot pray for himself, and possibly his senses fail and are gone, and the prayers of others can be but little refreshment, that even then he is reached by the benefit of Christ's intercession.

Fourth, consider God's covenant, and His love and

faithfulness in keeping covenant even in and through death. When David (2 Samuel 23:5) was about to comfort himself against death (which seems to be his scope in these words), he drew his comfort from the ground that God had made with him "an everlasting covenant, ordered in all things and sure." And the covenant helds forth five properties in God, that most strongly comfort against death:

• The love of God. That is stronger than death, for death will never overcome it, but it overcomes death. "Who shall separate us from the love of God?" said the apostle in Romans 8:37. "Shall tribulation, or distress, or persecution? Nay, in all these things, we are more than conquerors through Him that loved us." The love of God gets the victory, and gives the believer the victory over all not only in life, but in death, since it is of infinitely broad extent and of everlasting duration.

• The faithfulness of God. In this covenant the faithfulness of God is pledged to the believer, which death does not take away. Hence God is said to be the God not of the dead, but of the living. Though Abraham is dead, yet God is his God still; the covenant relation is not dissolved, but as He is faithful in keeping covenant with him while he is alive, so is He at death—which is the prefixed term for making all the promises of the covenant fully forthcoming, and for entering believers in possession of them.

• The wisdom of God. His wisdom is shown in framing the covenant so suitably that it comforts not only in life, but at death; therefore it is said to be ordered in all things. The promises of grace and mercy in the covenant are not only to give pardon here throughout the believer's life, but assured quietness at death, even though sense and feeling are gone.

• The justice of God. Though God's justice seems to be most terrible, yet is it comfortable to believers at death. "Henceforth is laid up for me," said the apostle in 2 Timothy 4:8, "a crown of righteousness, which God the righteous judge shall give to me at that day." For it is just with God to give to believers what Christ has bought and purchased at so dear a rate for them, to give them comfort who have taken themselves to Him for it; for though He gives nothing to believers on the account of their merit, yet there is a suitableness and proportionableness by which He walks towards them—and without all doubt Christ has merited those great things for them which God in justice is obliged to Him to bestow on them.

• The power of God. This is engaged to keep a believer's salvation (1 Peter 1:5). He has spoken the Word, and He can and will make it good. And there is nothing wherein His power shines forth more conspicuously than in their support and keeping in their death, when temptations are readily strongest.

Fifth, consider the operation and work of the Spirit of God. This may be considered either as His comfortable work, as He is the Spirit of adoption bearing witness with their spirits; or as it is His sanctifying and mortifying work, killing inward lusts; or as it is His strengthening or quickening work, whereby He keeps life in the believer, and gives him an earnest of that which is coming. The more of these he has, the more quietly and comfortably he may die. The seed of God is in him and is kept still alive in him. And, since God's providence, Christ's death, resurrection, intercession, and administration of His offices, God's covenant and all His properties, with the work of His Spirit, are all engaged for the believer, what more can be required for his comfortable support in death? And yet all these are God's allowance on him, even on everyone who has made his peace with God through Jesus Christ. Oh, are they not blessed then who die in the Lord?

Here, take some comfortable considerations since there are so many fruits that spring from these grounds, so many fruits of God's love and everlasting covenant. God gives charge to His angels to attend believers at death, as a convoy for their souls to the bosom of Abraham (Luke 16); for if angels are ministering spirits to page and wait on them in their life, they are much more so at their death. God is so tender of them that He has angels (more than one) waiting on them. And though this does not come up to the same level as the former grounds of comfort, springing more immediately from the Father, the Son, and the Holy Spirit, yet it is exceedingly comfortable, when neither minister nor friends can comfort, that they have glorious angels to be with them forever, to convoy them to heaven, which is by them accounted an honorable piece of service.

There is an immediate happiness wherewith the soul is possessed on the back of death, for it is immediately carried, as I said, to the bosom of Abraham, or rather to the bosom of Jesus Christ. The deceased believer has a perfect freedom from all ills of this life. There is no sin, no challenge, no accusation, no cross, no difficulty, no weight; all tears are wiped from their eyes; sorrow and sighing flee away, and they have absolute freedom from all the disquietness that is here in this life.

They are brought to the possession of their hope; they are brought to the immediate enjoyment of God and of Christ as a visible man. They are furnished with all desirable perfections; nothing is now in part, but all is perfect. They are perfect in knowledge, and have a clear resolution to all their doubts. Things which were disputed long about here with much contention, and which seldom came to a clear and satisfying close, a glance of God and of Christ fully satisfied all these.

There is an admission to all the privileges of heaven, a place given among them who stand by. They sit on thrones with Abraham, Isaac, Jacob, Moses, Samuel, David, and with the rest of the prophets; with Paul, James, John, and the rest of the apostles, where they behold the face of God and of the Lamb, and are among His attendants serving Him always without any the least weariness, weight, or burden, without any difficulty or indisposition, and blessing and praising Him forever and ever. And is not this a most heartsome and comfortable life and lot? May not a believer then yield to death, yea and make it very welcome on this ground, especially considering what a miserable world he lives in, and how eminently, abundantly, and superexcellently all the vain and vanishing shadows and shows here are made up by what is most real, solid, substantial, satisfying, and abiding there?

There is the resurrection of a believer's body. Though this tabernacle is dissolved and goes to the dust, yet it must rise up again. That part of Isaiah's song from chapter 26 is then eminently verified: "Thy dead men shall live, together with my dead body shall they arise; awake and sing ye that dwell in the dust, for their dew is as the dew of herbs, and the earth shall cast out the dead." As in winter the herbs are not seen, yet the roots remain in the ground, and they rise again in the spring, so (says faith, resting on the Word of promise) shall the bodies of the godly rise immortal, having agility and aptitude to follow the Lamb whithersoever He goes. These bodies that were sown in corruption and dishonor, and which after lying in the ground awhile, become very loathsome, shall be raised in incorruption and glory, even conformed to the glorious body of Jesus Christ. These bodies that were sown in weakness, even such weakness that they could not go on their own feet to the grave, nay, that were without all life, motion, sense, and feeling, shall be raised in power, as you may see at greater length in these excellently sweet and comfortable words of the apostle found in 1 Corinthians 15, wherein he not only clears the great truth of the resurrection, but also shows what grounds of comfort he and other believers had against death in it.

Last, consider what will be the case of souls and bodies when that desirable day of the resurrection comes, when these two old intimates shall meet together and renew their acquaintance again in much better condition than they parted. There will be no more wrestling thenceforth between flesh and spirit, but a holy harmony in a unified and joint enjoyment of God, in a unified and joint delighting in and serving God, and in a unified and joint satisfaction in God and being with God forevermore; for "we shall be forever with the Lord," said the apostle in 1 Thessalonians 4:17–18. "Wherefore," he says, "comfort one another with these words." Indeed, there is good and ground to do. Consider withal the great honor they will have at judgment, and the happiness following it.

To return then to what I proposed, seeing that believers in Christ have such pregnant and impregnable grounds to comfort them against death, seeing that such sweet and excellent fruits flow from these grounds, and since there is such a good begun at death that has no end, may they not be very quiet in their life and at their death, and be exceedingly comforted, whatever the time, the place, or the manner may be that God in His wisdom shall think fit to call them by death out of this present evil world?

Application

USE OF EXHORTATION TO BELIEVERS. First, lay up this comfort and, second, bless God for this comfort, that He has provided so very well for you in both this life, and at and after your death. Third, bless Him that He was ever graciously pleased to bring you to this happy condition, when He might have left you altogether comfortless both in life and death. Oh, bless Him that He has given His Son Jesus Christ, that He has come, and that grace through Him is extended so broadly as to take you in. It should make you cry with holy David in a transport of admiration, "What am I, and what is my father's house, that Thou hast brought me hitherto?" (2 Samuel 7:18), and with him to say, "I bless the Lord that hath given me counsel" (Psalm 16:7).

But there are two uses I would speak a little more particularly to, the first whereof, is to exhort you to that which is the sum of all I have spoken to you from these words, and that is to study to live so that you may die in Christ, which death has so many and so strong grounds of consolation awaiting it that all the world cannot possibly parallel or equal them. If there were no other motive to press you to faith in Christ, to mortification, and to making your calling and election sure, it should be sufficient that these things have such comforts at death and against it, which are the most incontrovertibly sure, stable, and lasting grounds of comfort. Other grounds of comfort go quite dry and vanish at death. They are but miserable comforters, and are like Job's winter brooks of water, that in summer disappoint the weary traveler and send him away ashamed. But these comforts can guard the heart against the law, against challenges for sin, and against the devil.

Nay, let us suppose that there are millions of devils, challenges for sin, and laws transgressed thereby, to speak and pass sentence against the believer in Christ. There is mighty and marvelous ground of comfort for him against them all here. He may appear and appeal and confidently say, "There are more with me than against me." Death to him lacks its sting and sin its strength, and he may step over the bounds and borders of time into eternity with a song of praise and triumph in his mouth, and die as quietly and confidently as if he were to lie down in his bed, as it is Isaiah 57:1–2; yea, with a great deal more quietness, confidence, and cheerfulness.

Therefore, were you to choose a way of living, let it be to live so that you may die in Christ. This is, as I said, the great scope of all that I have spoken from these words, even to stir you up to live so that you may be happy at your death, and that is to die in Him.

I shall propose but one consideration to enforce this upon you, and it is this: that way of living and dying has with it an alteration of the nature of all things. When a man is an enemy to God, all things are accused to him; but when he is friends with God and in good terms with Him, all things are blessed to him, and work together for his good (Romans 8:28)—and death comes in among these "all things." All things are yours, said the apostle in 1 Corinthians 3, "whether Paul, or Cephas, life, or death, things present, or things to come." They are all at your service; they are all yours as to the blessed use of them; they work together for your good, and prove all contributive and subservient to bringing you to glory.

USE OF INSTRUCTION. See what great prejudice you suffer, and what disadvantage you lie under, who do not live so as to die in Christ. You have not even the least of these consolations, and therefore, in the name of the Lord, ye are inhibited and discharged to meddle with them. See that none of you who resolve not to rest on Christ by faith, to live holily, and to show forth His praise by a shining and exemplary conversation, dare presume to put forth your hand to touch these consolations. That terrible word in Jeremiah 7:9–10 calls out for your consideration: "Will ye steal, murder, and commit adultery, and swear falsely, and come and stand before Me in this house, and say we are delivered to do all these abominations?" Will you take your own way of profane living, and yet expect any benefit from God's covenant, or any saving fruit of His grace? As God reckoned with profane Israel, so shall He reckon with you, and shall separate you from His people unto a curse, and the anger of God shall smoke against you. Not one graceless sinner shall be permitted to join himself to or lurk among the great company and congregation of the godly. Angels shall separate you from them, and the Judge shall separate you from Him and them with that doleful sentence, "Depart from Me, ye workers of iniquity." That sentence will be as terrible to you as the godly's sentence will be comfortable to them, "Come, ye blessed of My Father."

Take notice of this, all you who think you will die well (and no marvel, for so profane Balaam desired to die the death of the righteous), but have no care to live well. When all this doctrine is summed up, it will draw your happiness on this very hinge and bring it to this issue, whether you will indeed, in the Lord's strength, set yourselves to live so as to die in Christ, that in this case all these consolations, even all the consolations of the Gospel, shall be yours—but not one of them all is yours otherwise. To them who die in the Lord, and to them only, happiness is promised; but, on the contrary, to all them who do not live for Him and do not die in Him, God is an enemy in both life and death. His curse follows them here, and cleaves close to them like a girdle does to the loins of a man in the grave, so that they shall never be able to shake it off.

Sins and challenges shall then be multiplied; death shall then put forth its sting and sin its strength; the grave shall then obtain full victory over them; it shall feed on them. But it shall not be so with the godly. Death shall have no dominion over them as it has over the wicked who die in their sins and out of Christ. Death and the curse make a mortal, as it were, of all who live and die out of Christ; it eats them up and consumes them forevermore. When the first death is over and gone, the second death takes hold of them and never lets go of its hold. So death will still, even through all eternity, pursue the quarrel against them.

Therefore, let me close all I have said with two words. The first is to you who make conscience of being and living in Christ. Though you come short of that which you much covet and long to be, and that which is called for from you, which is your burden and affliction, yet consider what a comfortable allowance you have from God, who is the God of all consolation, and be comforted in it. Whatever your lot and condition in the world is, be what it will or may be, a little time will put it to an end. Therefore, I say, take encouragement from these grounds of consolation that God has given you against the terribleness of death, and walk so that you may not mar your own comfort. And withal, bless God, who has given you such a good ground of hope. You have more to make a truly comfortable life to you than all the kings and great men in the earth have who are outside of Christ. You may be sinfully defective in this much-called-for duty of blessing God, who has provided so well for you, and may rob Him of the glory that is infinitely due to Him from you, on many accounts, if you do not look to it.

The second word is to all of you whom I would earnestly beseech, for the Lord's sake, and, as you prize these mercies, to take the way that God has staked out to come by them. Dying in the Lord is the great qualification that has all these comforts annexed to it; and living in and to Him is the indispensably requisite qualification of all who would die in Him. This is to live by faith in the Son of God, and to live Christ-like; to live so that Christ may live in you and you in Him; that the truth and the straitness of your union with Him may be evident and apparent by the fruits of it. In a word, it is to live in continual communion with Him, and in the close and constant pursuit of conformity to Him.

I will dare to say to you who live so, yea, to all of you on condition that you will through grace choose this way of living, that you shall die happy; for the mouth of the Lord has spoken it, and will make it good: "Blessed are they which die in the Lord." He has pronounced blessedness on such in death and after death.

On the other hand, if you go the way of most, live carnally and carelessly, do not think more on death, and will do no more to prepare and make ready for it, alas, I must say to you, and dare not but say to you, and the Lord will ratify and confirm it, that you have nothing to do with these comforts of His people, nor do you have any part or portion in them. And if so, what do you have to comfort yourselves in, though you were all kings and queens, of the most opulent, potent, and flourishing kingdoms in the world? God will say to you that you had nothing to do but to take His covenant in your mouths, since you hated to be reformed.

And though, poor wretches, you now live in carnal mirth and jollity, yet your laughter and joy, your singing and dancing, shall by and by be turned into mourning, into weeping, wailing, and gnashing of teeth. As your mirth and laughter end, your weeping and howling shall begin, but never end. Is there not then, a vastly great difference between dying in sin and dying in Christ? And all this depends on your way of living. Is there not then a necessity, a most absolute and indispensable necessity, of your being in Him, and of your living in Him and to Him, if you would not, to your eternal prejudice and loss, be found mistaking or not duly considering these things that belong to your peace, till your day is over and gone, and matters between Him and you are past all remedy?

Now may the Lord Himself, who alone can do it, powerfully persuade and prevail with you so to live that you may have the well-grounded hope of dying in Christ, since blessed and only blessed are they who die in the Lord, who rest from their labors and whose works follow them.

Finis